Trichocosr

CW01064577

Notes historical, æsthetical, ~~~~~~~,

physiological, anecdotal and tonsorial

On the hair & beard

Anonymous

Alpha Editions

This edition published in 2024

ISBN : 9789362093110

Design and Setting By
Alpha Editions
www.alphaedis.com
Email - info@alphaedis.com

As per information held with us this book is in Public Domain.
This book is a reproduction of an important historical work. Alpha Editions uses the
best technology to reproduce historical work in the same manner it was first
published to preserve its original nature. Any marks or number seen are left
intentionally to preserve its true form.

BEAUTY OF THE HAIR.

CHAPTER I.

Although much time and attention are usually bestowed in dressing and ornamenting the hair, in compliance with the dictates of fashion, but little regard is paid to the natural beauty of the hair itself, as contributing to the expression and comeliness of the features. The absurdities and caprices of fashion have been constant themes for ridicule and declamation with the wits of all ages. The sharp epigrams of Martial, the satires of Juvenal, the anathemas of the Romish ecclesiastics, the invectives of sour Puritans, the coarse raillery of Swift, and the good humour of Addison, have all in turn been levelled against some prevailing folly of the day. It is not our intention, however, to act the part of censor, but, as humble chroniclers, to note the change from one fashion to another.

Before entering on the task we will say a few words about the hair, in relation to art, a subject of some interest, and which we believe has not been sufficiently insisted on. The hair is, undoubtedly, the chief ornament of the head; we naturally associate the idea of vigour, fertility, and gracefulness, with its growth. Its flowing outline gives grace and freedom to the symmetry of the features, and by a little license of the artist's hand, its form may be made to correct whatever harshness of character the countenance may chance to have acquired. In the colour, too, and texture of the hair, what facilities are afforded for heightening the charm of the most delicate complexion, or the dignity of the manly brow. The poets have universally recognised the truth of these principles, and in their descriptions of ideal beauty we invariably find some allusion to the hair.

Milton delights to adorn the human countenance with long hair, flowing in rich profusion. Of Eve he sings:

> "She, as a veil, down to the slender waist
>
> Her unadorned golden tresses wore
>
> Dishevelled, but in wanton ringlets waved
>
> As the vine curls her tendrils,——"

and to Adam he gives

> "Hyacinthine locks

Round from his parted forelock manly hung."

Even his angels are conspicuous for their beautiful hair—for instance

> "Of charming sunny rays a golden tiar
>
> Circled his head, nor less his locks behind
>
> Illustrious on his shoulders, fledge with wings,
>
> Lay waving round"——

The vivid descriptions of Homer, full of local colouring, afford many instances of the picturesque effect produced by duly noting so apparently a trivial matter, as the colour or crispness of the hair. Shakspere makes frequent allusions to its beauty: at the touch of his master hand a gleam of light seems to play about the silken tresses:

> "Here in her hairs
>
> The painter plays the spider, and hath woven
>
> A golden mesh to entrap the hearts of men!"

The Italian poets also show the same love of the beautiful, and fondness for

> "Le crespe chiome d'or puro lucente."

How much the form and variety of the hair help to distinguish the style and character of a composition was well understood by the ancient sculptors and painters. "The hair of the Phidian Jove, in the Vatican, rises in spouts, as it were, from the forehead, and then falls in waving curls, like the mane of the lion, most majestic and imperial in appearance. The crisp curls of Hercules again remind us of the short locks between the horns of the indomitable bull; whilst the hair of Neptune falls down wet and dank, like his own sea-weed. The beautiful flowing locks of Apollo, full and free, represent perpetual youth; and the gentle, vagrant, bewitching tresses of Venus, denote most clearly her peculiar characters and claims as a divinity of Olympus." We remark the same peculiarity in the portraits by Sir Peter Lely of the court beauties of the time of Charles II.

> "Loves walks the pleasant mazes of the hair."

Hair is to the human aspect what foliage is to the landscape; and, whenever pen or pencil is guided by poetic feeling or good taste, it lingers with admiration and delight amid the shadows and glossy silken sheen—the ever-varying tints, and waving, wanton loveliness of sunny, luxuriant hair. Indeed, so beautiful is the hair itself, when arranged with taste, and kept in good order, (that is in a growing, healthful state,) that the addition of any further ornament, by way of head-dress, is all but superfluous. Not that all ornament should be dispensed with, but that great judgment is necessary in selecting such as correct taste may approve. Addison, with his usual good sense, thus counsels his fair readers: "I would desire the fair sex to consider how impossible it is for them to add anything that can be ornamental to what is already the masterpiece of nature. The head has the most beautiful appearance, as well as the highest station, in the human figure. Nature has laid out all her art in beautifying the face; she has touched it with vermilion, planted in it a double row of ivory, made it the seat of smiles and blushes, lightened it up and enlivened it with the eyes, hung it on each side with curious organs of sense, given it airs and graces which cannot be described, and surrounded it with such a flowing shade of hair as sets its beauties in the most agreeable light. In short, she seems to have designed the head as a cupola to the most glorious of her works; and when we load it with such a pile of supernumerary ornaments, we destroy the symmetry of the human figure, and foolishly contrive to call off the eye from great and real beauties to childish gew-gaws, ribbons, and bone lace."

And beautiful exceedingly are those beloved memorials—the silken locks of childhood, the treasured tresses of riper years, or the silver gray of reverend old age—which, in the eyes of sorrowing friends, are the dearest relics of the loved ones whose angel spirits beyond the tomb have passed through death into eternity.

> "There seems a love in hair, though it be dead:
>
> It is the gentlest, yet the strongest thread
>
> Of our frail plant—a blossom from the tree
>
> Surviving the proud trunk; as if it said,
>
> Patience and Gentleness in Power. In me
>
> Behold affectionate eternity."

Leigh Hunt.

THE FASHION OF ANTIQUITY.

CHAPTER II.

The fashion of ornamenting the hair is an universal vanity, probably as old as the creation; for the earliest records and antiquities introduce us to the mysteries of wigs and beard cases, and such evident and lavish displays of tonsorial art, as remind one more of the skilful artist than the first rude essays of the craft. It has been suggested by a writer in the *Quarterly Review* that we are indebted to Eve herself for the first principles of the art, and that probably by the reflection in some tranquil stream she made her earliest studies.

In the sculptures from Nineveh we have an exact representation of the fashion of the hair among the Assyrians—thousands of years before Britain had a place in history. The office of *coiffeur* in those days must evidently have been one of no little importance. From the king on the throne—the mighty hunter, lion slayer, and destroyer of men—his counsellors, and great captains, to the poor slave, the mere hewer of wood and drawer of water, all seem to have passed under the discipline of the curling-irons. The curling and plaiting of the beard and hair, as shown in the sculptures, is doubtless intended as a distinguishing mark of a superior and conquering race. Their colossal-winged bulls and monstrous deities are adorned with the same venerable badge of power and authority. Since nearly all that is known on this subject is directly derived from the researches of Mr. Layard, we cannot do better than refer to the volumes of one to whom not only this nation, but the civilised world, are indebted for his arduous and most successful explorations.

"The Assyrians paid particular attention to the adorning of their persons. Besides wearing numerous ornaments, they most carefully and elaborately platted their hair and beards. The hair was parted over the forehead, and fell from behind the ears on the shoulders in a large bunch of ringlets. The beard was allowed to grow to its full length, and, descending low on the breast, was divided into two or three rows of curls. The moustache was also carefully trimmed and curled at the ends. The hair, as well as the beard, appears to have been dyed, as is still the custom in Persia; but it has been doubted whether the hair, represented in the sculptures, was natural or artificial.

"According to Herodotus (Lib. 1, c. 195) the Babylonians wore their hair long. The great regularity of the curls in the sculptures would certainly lead to the impression that part of the hair, at least, was false; but we can scarcely suppose that the warriors, as well as the king and the principal officers of state, wore false beards, for all the sculptured beards are equally elaborate and studied in the arrangement. The mode of representing hair in the bas-reliefs is most probably conventional. Most Eastern people have been celebrated for the length and beauty of their hair, and if the Assyrians were as well provided with it as the inhabitants of Persia were in the days of Darius, or as they now are, they would have had little occasion for a wig."

The hair of females, in the sculptures, is usually represented in long ringlets, sometimes plaited and braided, and at other times confined in a net. The modern fashion of wearing the hair in a net is therefore a revival of a very ancient one. Isaiah alludes to "the caps of net-work," (chap. III., v. 8).

It is to ancient Egypt we must look for the earliest instance of a people investing themselves with that symbol of wisdom and gravity—the wig. It was reserved for the courtiers of Louis XIII. to re-introduce and remodel the ancient perruque, but its origin certainly dates from a very remote antiquity. The Egyptians as a nation were "all shaven and shorn:" they shaved even the heads of young children, leaving only certain locks as an emblem of youth. All classes among the people, the slaves imported from foreign countries not excepted, were compelled to submit to the tonsure. The universal custom of shaving the head led to the use of wigs. "It may appear singular," says Wilkinson, "that so warm a covering to the head should have been adopted in the climate of Egypt; but we must recollect the reticulated texture of the ground-work, on which the hair was fastened, allowed the heat of the head to escape, while the hair effectually protected it from the sun: it is evident that no better covering could have been devised, and that it far surpassed, in comfort and coolness, the modern turban." Wigs were worn both within the house and out of doors, like the turban of the present day. A wig in the British Museum, from the temple of Isis, and one in the Berlin Museum, still attest the skill of the Egyptian artist. For the use of those who could not afford the more expensive wigs of real hair, an imitation appears to have been made of wool and other stuffs. A most singular custom of the Egyptians was that of tying a false beard upon the chin, which was made of plaited hair, and of a peculiar form, according to the rank of the person by whom it was worn. Private individuals had a small beard, scarcely two inches long; that of a king was of considerable length, square at the bottom; and the figure of gods were distinguished by its turning up at the ends. The women always wore their hair long and plaited. The back part was made to consist of a number of strings of hair, reaching to the shoulder-blades, and on each side other strings of the same descended over the breast. The hair was plaited in the triple plait, the ends being left loose, or, more usually, two or three plaits were fastened together at the extremity by woollen strings of corresponding colour. Many of the mummies of women have been found with the hair perfectly preserved, plaited in the manner described, the only alteration in its appearance being the change of its black hue, which became reddened by exposure to great heat, during the process of embalming.

The Hebrews wore their hair generally short, and checked its growth by the application of scissors only. They seem at an early period to have availed themselves of the assistance of art, not only for beautifying the hair, but increasing its thickness; while the heads of the priests were anointed with an unguent of a peculiar kind. The custom of anointing the head became a general mark of gentility, and an essential part of the daily toilet. The Lawgiver of the Jews did not think it beneath the dignity of his code to introduce into it an especial ordinance concerning the fashion of the beard— "Thou shalt not mar the corners of the beard"—(Leviticus XIX., v. 27). By the "corners" the commentators understand the extremities; and this precept, no doubt, like others in the same chapter, arose from the leading policy of the theocracy, which sought to create a people in everything distinct from, and unmixed with, the idolators by whom they were surrounded.

It was the noble destiny of the Greeks to add beauty and refinement to the creations and speculations of a previous age. The love of the beautiful was a passion with the Greeks; it was stamped, so to speak, on the meanest objects of every-day life, and found its loftiest expression in their poetry and the magnificent works of art, which every civilized people regard as models for imitation. Even in the mere matter of a head-dress, we are struck with the beauty of the classic forms in Greek sculpture, which show a rare perception of the beautiful, in wonderful contrast to the barbarism of earlier, and, we may add, succeeding ages. In Homer the Greeks are repeatedly spoken of as the "long-haired Greeks," and to almost every character in the Iliad and Odyssey some epithet is applied in allusion to the beauty of the hair. It is enough to allude to the fair-haired Helen, the nymph Calypso, Circe, and Ariadne; the flowing locks of Achilles, the curls of Paris, and the auburn hair of Ulysses. It will be remembered that Achilles made sacrifice of his yellow hair at the funeral pyre of Patroclus, in honour of the friend he loved.

The ancient practice of wearing the hair long was adhered to for many centuries by the Spartans. The Spartan boys always had their hair cut quite short; but, as soon as they reached the age of puberty, they let it grow long. They prided themselves upon their hair, and called it the cheapest of ornaments. Before engaging in battle, they combed and dressed their hair with much care, as did Leonidas and his followers at Thermopylae.

The custom of the Athenians was different. They wore their hair long in childhood; but the youths cut off their flowing locks at a certain age, and, as a religious ceremony, consecrated them to some god: on attaining the age of manhood, they again let the hair grow. In ancient times at Athens the hair was rolled up in a kind of knot on the crown of the head, and fastened with golden clasps in the shape of grasshoppers. The Athenian females, also, wore the hair much in the same fashion. It was usually confined in a net-work of silk or gold thread, or a cap or turban of close material, and, at times, by broad bands of cloth of different colours wound round the head.

The Greek philosophers were distinguished by their majestic beards, and Socrates, it would seem, pre-eminently so. Homer's description of the venerable beards of Nestor and Priam is doubtless familiar to most readers. The Greeks wore their beards till the time of Alexander; and Plutarch mentions that the beards of the Macedonian soldiers were cut off to prevent the enemy from seizing hold of them in battle.

Pliny says that the Romans wore their hair long till the year 454 A.U.C., when P. Ticinius Mena first introduced a number of barbers from Sicily. Those bearded ancestors of the Romans, with their long hair, came, in after times, to be regarded with no little reverence, as the true type of manly virtue and integrity, "the fine old *Roman* gentleman." At the time of the invasion of the Gauls, Livy tells us, as the soldiers entered Rome, they were struck with awe and astonishment at the noble beards and venerable aspect of the old magnates seated at their thresholds; and, that a soldier venturing, out of mere curiosity, but to touch the beard of one of them, the affront was resented by a blow with his ivory sceptre, which was the signal for a general slaughter.

The hair was usually worn short and crisp till the time of Commodus, who was particularly luxurious in the dressing and ornamenting of his hair, which was powdered with gold. Having, however, a somewhat uneasy conscience, he resorted to the singular practice of burning off the beard, "timore tonsoris," says Lampridius.

Scipio Africanus first set the example of shaving. Persons of quality had their children shaved for the first time by a person of the same or greater quality, who, by this means, became godfather or adopted father of the children. The day was observed as one of rejoicing, and the hair of the beard made an offering to some god. The beard of Nero, we are told, was put into a golden box adorned with pearls, and consecrated in this way to Jupiter Capitolinus. Hadrian was the first emperor who wore a beard; Plutarch says he wore it to hide the scars in his face. Constantine was distinguished by the title of "Pogoniatos;" and we should do injustice to Julian's beard to omit mention of it here. Gibbon says, "the Emperor had been insulted by satires and libels; and, in his turn, composed, under the title of the 'Enemy of the Beard,' an ironical confession of his own faults, and a severe satire on the licentious and effeminate manners of Antioch." He descants with seeming complacency on his own "shaggy and *populous beard*"—a phrase which we may interpret literally or not, as we please. The historian adds, "This imperial reply was publicly exposed before the gates of the palace, and the MISOPOGON remains a singular monument of the resentment, the wit, the humanity, and the indiscretion of Julian." Probably no nation ever patronized the tonsor with more assiduity than Rome in the decadence of the Empire. The young patrician exquisites of those days devoted hours daily to the barber and the bath; and no lady's train of slaves was complete without the *ornatrix*, whose duty it was to attend the toilet of her mistress, for the special purpose of dressing her hair.

An elegant simplicity at one time characterized the head-dress of the Roman ladies, who generally adopted the fashion of the Greeks, which usually, however, soon degenerated into extravagance and coarseness. They piled upon their heads imitations of castles and crowns, cumbrous wreaths, and other absurdities, and knotted the hair with tiresome minuteness.

> "With curls on curls they build their head before,
>
> And mount it with a formidable tower:
>
> A giantess she seems, but look behind;
>
> And then she dwindles to the pigmy kind."

The *calamistrum* or curling irons, had a busy time of it, for the craving after novelty was intense, and any artificial arrangement of the hair welcomed as a change.

> "More leaves the forest yields not from the trees,
>
> Than there be fashions of attire in view,
>
> For each succeeding day brings something new."

Poppea, Nero's wife, was so conspicuous for the beauty of her hair, that he composed a poem in honour of it.

It was the custom of the Romans to let their beard and hair grow during the period of mourning; as we are informed by Suetonius, Augustus did his, after the terrible Varian catastrophe. The slaves had the hair cut close as a mark of servitude. Wigs and false hair were worn by the Romans, more especially by the females; thus Martial——

> "The golden hair which Galla wears
>
> Is her's—who would have thought it?
>
> She swears 'tis hers; and true she swears,

For I know where she bought it!"

Juvenal describes Messalina putting on a wig of flaxen hair to conceal her own black locks when she left the palace in disguise:

"Et nigrum flavo crinem abscondente galero."

Among the Gauls (Gallia comata) long and flowing hair was greatly esteemed. Cæsar says that he always ordered the long hair of the conquered races to be shaved off, in submission to the Roman arms; and, during the decline of the empire, whenever a province revolted, the patriot leaders urged the adoption of the opposite fashion of wearing long hair, as a mark of freedom and independence. Thus the fashion of the hair, as in later times, had a political significance, and took part in revolutions and the great struggles for social freedom.

FREAKS OF FASHION.

CHAPTER III.

We will now conduct the reader, who has condescended to accompany us thus far, through the succeeding centuries and complete our illustrations of the fashion of bygone times.

Cæsar describes the Britons as having long flowing hair, and a beard on the upper lip only. A bust in the British Museum, one of the Townley marbles, supposed by some to represent Caractacus, may be taken as a good example of the fashion of hair worn by the British chieftains. The hair is parted along the crown of the head, and disposed on each side of the face and down in the neck in thick bold masses. Immense tangled moustaches, reaching sometimes to the breast, completed the hirsute ornaments of the tattooed Briton. Strabo says, in his time the inhabitants of the Scilly Islands had long beards, like goats. Dion Cassius alludes to the long yellow hair of Boadicea flowing over her shoulders, which sufficiently indicates the *coiffure* of that undaunted heroine.

The Anglo Saxons considered fine hair as the most becoming of personal ornaments, and took every pains to dress it to the greatest advantage. Aneurin, the Welch bard, says, the warriors wore a profusion of hair, and were as proud of it as the women, decking it with beads and ornaments. It was worn long, and parted on the forehead, falling naturally on the shoulders; the beard of ample growth, and forked. To have the hair cut entirely off was considered a great disgrace—a mode of punishment inflicted upon criminals. Adhelm, bishop of Sherbone, who wrote in the eighth century, describes a maiden as having her locks delicately curled by the iron of those adorning her. The clergy were obliged to shave the crowns of their heads, and to keep their hair short to distinguish them from the laity. Again and again the denunciations of the clergy were directed against the practice of wearing long hair, but with partial results; the old Teutonic love of flowing locks was too strong to be extinguished by the threatenings of the Church.

When the Gauls were ruled by native sovereigns, none but nobles and priests were allowed to wear long beards. A close shaven chin was a mark of servitude. In the days of Charlemagne, kings rivalled each other in the length and majesty of their beards. Eginhard, secretary to Charlemagne, describes the old race of kings as coming to the Field of Mars in a carriage drawn by oxen, and sitting on the throne with their flowing beards and dishevelled locks. So sacred a thing was a king's beard, that three of the hairs enclosed in the seal of a letter or charter were considered the most solemn pledge a king could offer.

The Danes, like the Anglo Saxons, took great pride in their hair; and the English women, we are told, were not a little captivated with some Danish officers, who especially delighted in combing and tending their hair: and we read of one Harold with the fair locks, whose thick ringlets reached to his girdle.

The Normans, at the time of the Conquest, not only shaved the upper lip and the entire face, but also cropped close or shaved the back of the head. Harold's spies, unacquainted with so singular a custom, on the approach of the Conqueror's forces, reported that his army was composed of priests, and not soldiers. Holinshed states that after the Conquest the English were ordered to shave their beards and round their hair, after the Norman fashion. When William returned to Normandy, he took with him some young Englishmen, as hostages: the French greatly admired their long beautiful curls. The Normans and Flemings, who accompanied the Conqueror, were too solicitous about their good looks to be long restricted to the stunted growth prescribed by military rule. All classes soon indulged in the forbidden luxury, and, as is usually the case, the reaction was extreme; so much so, that William of Malmesbury who makes complaint of the cropping of his countrymen in the previous reign, reprobates the immoderate length of the hair in the time of Rufus.

The prevailing sin of unshorn locks and curled moustaches had long been a grievous scandal in the eyes of the clergy. Councils were held at Limoges, in 1031; by Gregory VII. in 1073, and again at Rouen in 1095; on this much discussed grievance. Anselm, archbishop of Canterbury refused his benediction to those who would not cut their hair. And Serlo, bishop of Seez, when Henry was in Normandy, seems to have taken the matter literally into his own hands. Observing that the king and courtiers were moved by his zeal and eloquence, when preaching against this extravagant profusion of hair, he pulled out a pair of scissors, and docked the whole congregation, king and all, on the spot. A royal edict to the like effect was immediately issued. St. Wulstan, bishop of Worcester, took a somewhat singular method of enforcing his commands. When anyone knelt to receive his blessing, he would snip off a lock of their hair, throwing it in their face, and bidding them to cut off the rest, or perish in perdition.

The effigies of Henry and his Queen Matilda, at Rochester Cathedral, show the style of hair worn in those days. The king is represented with the beard trimmed round, and hair flowing in carefully-twisted ringlets upon his shoulders and down his back. The queen's hair descends in two long plaits to the hips, and terminates in small curls. These plaits were sometimes encased in silk, and bound round with ribbon.

Whatever changes were effected by the zeal of the clergy, it is certain that the fops in Stephen's reign had not conformed to their teachings. Historians describe their effeminate ringlets: and when these were not sufficiently ample, recourse was had to false hair.

In France, the denunciations of the clergy were as little heeded as in England. Louis VII., however, sacrificed his hair to save his conscience; he shaved himself as close as a monk, and disgusted his pleasure-loving queen, Eleanor of Guienne, by his denuded aspect and asceticism. Eleanor bestowed her favors upon another, was divorced, and subsequently gave her hand and dower—the fair provinces of Guienne and Poitou—to Henry, duke of Normandy, afterwards king of England—the first of the Plantaganets. In Henry's reign the old Norman custom, of shaving the beard closely, was revived.

During the absence of Richard Cœur de Lion, closely trimmed hair and shaven faces were the fashion; but, towards the close of this reign, short beards and moustaches reappeared.

In king John's reign curled hair was so much the fashion, that the beaux seldom appeared with any covering on their head, that their flowing locks might be everywhere admired. The king himself, and the nobles of his party, wore beard and moustaches, out of contempt, it is said, for the discontented barons. His effigy in Worcester Cathedral has the beard closely trimmed, and moustaches.

Curls and a shaven face, denote the gentlemen in the days of Henry III.; the ladies wear the hair turned up and confined in a caul.

Crispness of the hair and beard (which was curled with the nicest care) was the favourite fashion at the court of Edward Longshanks. His successor, as we may judge from the effigy at Gloucester, wore the beard carefully curled, and the hair cut square on the forehead, which hung in wavy ringlets below the ears. Can it be true that the beard of this wretched king suffered the indignity we read of in history? Did Maltravers order the king to be shaven with cold water from a dirty puddle, while on a journey near Carnarvon; and the poor king,

> "Fallen, fallen, fallen, fallen,
>
> Fallen from his high estate,"

bursting into tears exclaim, "Here at least is warm water on my cheeks, whether you will or not." Beards at that time were seldom worn but by aged persons, officers of state, and knights templars.

Edward III. on his tomb at Westminster, is figured with a noble beard, which would not have disgraced the chin of some old Greek in the heroic ages.

In Richard the Second's reign, we notice the hair of the ladies caught up prettily in a gold fret or caul, the hair usually surmounted by some ornament in jewelry, in the form of a chaplet, as described by Chaucer:

> "And everich on her head
>
> A rich fret of golde, which withouden drede
>
> Was full of stately net stones set,
>
> And every lady had a chapelet."

The king, as appears from his effigy, wore flowing curls, confined by a narrow fillet round the temple; his beard and moustache short, from which two small tufts depended on each side of the chin. The "Canterbury Tales" furnish admirable sketches by a master-hand in illustration of our subject. The squire, "a lover and a lusty bachelor," is pictured "with lockés curl'd as they were laid in press;" the franklin had a beard

> "White was his beard as is the dayesy;"

the merchant—

> "A merchant was there with a forked beard;"

and the sumpnour,

> "With sealled browes, black and pilled beard.'
>
> The *Pardoner* had hair as yellow as wax,
>
> But smooth it hung, as doth a strike of flax;
>
> By ounces hung his lockés that he had,
>
> And therewith he his shoulders overspread,
>
> Full thin it lay by culpons, on and on.

*****

> No beard had he, no ever none should have,
>
> As smooth it was as it were newe shave."

The "shipman," we know not if he had "the long gray beard, and glittering eye," of The Ancient Mariner, but

> "With many a tempest had his beard been shaken;"

the miller's beard,

> "As any sow or fox, was red,
>
> And thereto broad, as though it were a spade;"

and the Reve—

> "The Revé was a choleric man,
>
> His head was shav'd as nigh as ever he can;
>
> His hair was by his earés round yshorn;
>
> His top was decked like a priest beforn."

But here we must part company with the pilgrims, and proceed on our way.

During the reign of Henry IV., there occurred a marked change of fashion; the hair was now closely cropped round the head. The king retained the beard and moustaches; but, his successor, Henry V., discarded them, and, in his reign, even military men seldom wore moustaches, and none but old men had beards. A kind of horned head-dress was in favour with females, which Lydgate, the monk of Bury, ridicules:

> "Horns were given to beasts for defence;
>
> A thing contrary to feminity—

but "feminity" heeded not.

Men's faces were all closely shaven in the time of Henry VII.; and certain turban-like and heart-shaped head-dresses, worn by females, were now of such unusual width, that we are told the doors of the palace at Vincennes had to be altered to admit the Queen of Charles VII., Isabella of Bavaria, when in full dress. At Paris, the horned head-dresses were doomed to perish in the flames. In 1429, a famous cordelier, one Thomas Conecte, preached in the church of St. Genevieve, for nine days in succession, to some thousands of auditors, against the pomps and vanities of this wicked world;

and, in a fit of enthusiasm, fires were lighted, the men flung their dice and cards into the flames, and the women their monstrous head-dresses, tails, and other articles of finery. A somewhat similar head-dress, however, survives to this day among the peasantry about Rouen, Caen, &c.; and the steeple head-dress of the fifteenth century is exactly represented by the *Cauchoise*, still worn in Normandy.

Again in the reign of Edward IV., another change occurs, and the hair is suffered to hang in profusion over the ears in large thick masses, called "side locks," covering the forehead, and drooping over the eyes in a very awkward manner—a fashion which scarcely varied during the remaining years of the Plantaganets.

Leland, in his description of the pageants at the marriage of Elizabeth to Henry VII., relates how the Queen was royally apparelled, "her fair yellow hair hanging down plain behind her back, with a caul (or net-work) of pipes over it, and a circlet of gold, richly garnished with precious stones, upon her head." To wear the hair at full length on the shoulders was the approved fashion for a bride—Anne Boleyn was so attired at her nuptials—and the fashion was very generally followed by unmarried females. The men vied with the fair sex in the length of their flowing curls, and the dandies, especially, loaded their shoulders with a rich profusion. Louis XII. of France had a very magnificent *chevelure*, till disease compelled him to take refuge in a wig.

It is almost as needless to say ought of "bluff king Hal," as to describe the current coin of the realm. He is a sort of Blue Beard, and the tragical story of his wives is known to everybody. He it was, who, in his royal will and pleasure, issued a peremptory order that the heads of his attendants and courtiers should be polled. We may be sure that short crops were soon in fashion. The Venetian ambassador at the English court writes, that when Henry heard that the king of France wore a beard, he allowed his, also, to grow, which, being somewhat red, had the appearance of golden hair. Henry was then about twenty-nine years of age.

Francis the First, who was wounded in a tournament, had to submit to the loss of his locks; so the pliant courtiers parted with theirs, which set the fashion of cropping the hair very close.

We have seen how bishops, in olden time, laid violent hands on their flocks, and imposed penalties on the laity, for too successfully cultivating their curls. But the sight of a bishop in danger of being shaved by his colleagues is a curiosity. We give the story as we find it in Southey's "Omniana:" "Guillaume

Duprat, bishop of Clermont, who assisted at the council of Trent, and built the college of the Jesuits at Paris, had the finest beard that ever was seen. It was too fine a beard for a bishop; and the canons of his cathedral, in full chapter assembled, came to the barbarous resolution of shaving him. Accordingly, when next he came to the choir, the dean, the *prevot*, and the *chantre* approached with scissors and razors, soap, basin, and warm water. He took to his heels at the sight, and escaped to his castle of Beauregard, about two leagues from Clermont, where he fell sick, from vexation, and died."

Hastening onward, we come to the days of good Queen Bess—and foremost is the figure of the queen herself—

"The cynosure of neighbouring eyes."

This was an age ever memorable for the choicest wits, and, we need not scruple to add, BEARDS. These were of every variety of cut, size, and colour; and certain professions were distinguished by particular beards. The cathedral beard, long and square-trimmed, which fell upon the breast, was worn by divines of the English church; the broad spade-beards and steeletto beards by soldiers: the former in favour with the Earl of Essex, the latter with Lord Southampton. There were, likewise, hammer-shaped beards, like the Roman T, similar to the formidable beard of the present Emperor of France; the *pique devant*, forked, needle, and tile-shaped beard; and round, trimmed beards, "like a glover's paring-knife."

Taylor, the Water-Poet, who had a curious cork-screw beard of his own, in his "Whip for Pride," thus flagellates the whole race:

Now a few lines to paper I will put,

Of men's beards strange and variable cut;

In which there's some do take as vain a pride

As almost in all other things beside.

Some are reaped most substantial as a brush,

Which make a natural wit known by the bush.

Some seem as they were starched stiff and fine,

Like to the bristles of some hungry swine;

And some (to set their love's desire on edge)

Are cut and pruned like a quick-set hedge.

Some like a spade, some like a fork, some square,

Some round, some mowed like stubble, some stark bare;

Some sharp stiletto-fashion, dagger-like,

That may, with whispering, a man's eye out pike;

Some with the hammer cut, or Roman T,

Their beards extravagant reformed must be;

Some with the quadrate, some triangle fashion,

Some circular, some oval in translation,

Some perpendicular in longitude,

Some like a thicket for their crassitude;

That heights, depths, breadths, triform, square, round,

And rules geometrical, in beards are found;

Besides the upper lip's strange variation,

Corrected from mutation to mutation;

As 'twere from tithing unto tithing sent,

Pride gives Pride continual punishment.

Some (spite their teeth) like thatch'd eaves downward grows,

And some grow upwards in despite their nose.

Some their mustachios of such length do keep,

That very well they may a manger sweep!

Which in beer, ale, or wine, they drinking plunge,

And suck the liquor up as 'twere a sponge;

But 'tis a sloven's beastly Pride, I think,

To wash his beard when other men may drink.

And some (because they will not rob the cup)

Their upper chaps like pot-hooks are turned up.

The Barbers, thus, (like Tailors) still must be

Acquainted with each cuts variety.

The word beard, in former times, was understood to comprehend what we now distinguish as beard, whiskers and moustaches. The colour of the beard was considered of much importance, and dyed, when needful, of the desired hue. Bottom, who was to act the part of Pyramus, "a most gentleman-like man," says, "I will discharge it in either your straw-coloured beard, your orange-tawny beard, your purple-in-grain beard, or your French-crown-colour beard, your perfect yellow," nor must we omit the most venerable of all, "a sable silvered." There was, also, the yellow, or Cain-coloured beard; and the red, or Judas-beard, formerly supposed to indicate a treacherous nature.

Beards of very noble proportions were worn at the era of the Reformation. We may instance Calvin, Beza, Peter Martyr, Fox, Cranmer, and John Knox, whose beard reached to his girdle. Possibly this length of beard was encouraged as much out of opposition to the Romish church, as from any real reverence for so patriarchal a fashion. Sully's or Lord Burleigh's beard may be taken as the finest growth to which statesmen have attained. The poets Spencer, Shakspere, and Beaumont, present fine patterns for their tuneful brethren; and scholars, if they despair of acquiring the erudition of a Scaliger, a Buchanan, or a Buxtorf, may resemble these old worthies in their plenitude of beard. Every painter is familiar with glorious old Titian's beard, with Reuben's and Vandyke's.

And looking back through the vistas of past ages, the monarchs of the intellectual world are, for the most part, distinguishable by their handsome beards. Henry the Fourth, of France, could boast of a splendid beard; but his successor, Louis XIII., was without, and the pliant courtiers, in deference to the smooth face of royalty, gave up wearing beards. Sully, however, retained his, much to the amusement of some jesting spirits about the court. The old man, indignant at such treatment, observed to the king, "Sire, your father, of glorious memory, when he wished to consult me on state affairs, bade the fools and jesters leave his presence."

Sir Thomas More's beard but narrowly escaped the stroke of the axe which ended the career of that illustrious man. The story is told thus: Sir Thomas More at his execution, having laid his head upon the block, and perceiving that his beard was extended in such a manner that it would be cut through by the stroke of the executioner, asked him to adjust it properly upon the block; and when the executioner told him he need not trouble himself about his beard, when his head was about to be cut off, "It is of little consequence to me," said Sir Thomas, "but it is a matter of some importance to you that you should understand your profession, and not cut through my beard, when you had orders only to cut off my head."

Ulmus of Padua wrote a folio volume on the Beard, as he well might, if the length of his discourse were proportioned to the noble beards it was his privilege to illustrate, and the dignity and gravity of the subject he had to discuss. Hotoman wrote a "Treatise," and Pierius Valerianus an "Eulogium" on beards. Those of Italy and Spain alone are worthy of a separate treatise. Many an Arab would rather lose his head than part with his beard—it is part of his religion to honour it; he swears by his beard: and Mahommed, we are told, never cut his. In Spain, in old times, it was held in like reverence: an insult to the beard could only be wiped out with blood. The seated corpse of the Cid—so runs the story—knocked down a Jew who dared to offend against its majesty by touching but a hair of the beard. It was reserved for the pencil of Velasquez to give immortality to the martial beards of Spain, which flourished proudly, and grew fiercely, amid the strife and smoke of battles. The decline and fall of the Spanish beard is attributed to Philip V. and his courtiers, in whose reign it was abolished. Many a brave Spaniard felt the privation keenly; and it became a common saying, "Since we have lost our beards, we seem to have lost our souls."

The Longobardi, or Lombards, have made themselves a place in history; and stubborn enough they proved at times, as Frederic I., the renowned old Barbarossa, found to his cost. And was there not the terrible Blue Beard—that incarnation of villainy and bloodthirstiness of our childhood. Who has forgotten the beards of the Persian kings, interwoven with gold; or the long white beard of the old Laconian mentioned by Plutarch, who being asked why he let it grow so long, replied, "It is that seeing continually my white beard, I may do nothing unworthy of its whiteness?" Fuller, however, says, "Beard was never the true standard of brains;" nor of valour either, if we may trust Bassanio:

> "How many cowards, whose hearts are all as false
>
> As stairs of sand, wear yet upon their chins
>
> The beards of Hercules and frowning Mars;
>
> Who inward search'd, have livers white as milk;
>
> And these assume but valour's excrement,
>
> To render them redoubted."

There seems, at all times to have been a sinister protest, in some quarter or other, against the presumed arrogance of the beard—a lurking spirit of revolt, engendered possibly of envy, against the supremacy of its reign. Even the would-be-philosopher of old did not go unchallenged, as we may guess from the sharp rebuke administered in the memorable words, "Video barbam et palliam; philosophum nondum video." And, indeed, if the truth must be spoken, there are faces to which it lends no dignity. A mean and contemptible nature, hid behind a potent beard, is a miserable disguise. The affectations of a gentleman are but trifles. Raleigh wore stays, and was a great dandy; but he was something more—an elegant poet, an accomplished gentleman, and a gallant soldier. But the abuse of a good thing is no argument for its disuse. We grieve to think of the degradation of this manly ornament, and put no faith in

> "those ambiguous things that ape
>
> Goats in their visage, women in their shape;"

and would fain hope that a return to the "flat faces,"

> "such as would disgrace a screen,"

is next to impossible.

> "Now, a beard is a thing which commands in a king,
>
> > Be his sceptre ne'er so fair;
>
> When the beard wears the sway, the people obey,
>
> > And are subject to a hair.

> "'Tis a princely sight and a grave delight
>
> > That adorns both young and old;
>
> A well thatch'd face is a comely grace,
>
> > And a shelter from the cold."

Even our playing cards look the better for the beards; how richly are the kings furnished—what a winning aspect it gives them.

> "Behold four kings, in majesty revered,
>
> With hoary whiskers and a forked beard."

When the lively Beatrice exclaims, "I could not endure a husband with a beard on his face," and is reminded she may light on one without, the alternative seems by no means pleasing; for she replies, "What shall I do with him? dress him with my apparel, and make him my waiting gentleman? He that hath a beard is more than a youth, and he that hath none is less than a man." And we take it, though the lady tells us she was born to speak "all mirth, no matter" she has given expression to the opinion of her own sex very naively. It was one of those consistent contradictions so in character with the delightful absurdities of lovers, for some sighing swains to part with "the old ornament of their cheeks;" some say, to give a more youthful appearance to those who stood in need of it; and adopted by others from the merciful consideration which swayed the heart of Bottom, when he resolved "to roar like a sucking dove," not to "fright the ladies." When the repentant Benedick turned lover, his beard was fated to stuff tennis-balls. To pluck a hair from the beard of the great Cham, at the bidding of some fair inamorata, was obviously an easy and agreeable duty to the knights of old romance. But what shall we say to those giants' coats

"Made from the beards of kings."

Once upon a time, by the exigencies of war, John de Castro was compelled to leave one of his whiskers in pledge with the inhabitants of Goa, as security for a thousand pistoles, which he needed to carry on the siege. A general's whiskers valued at 2,000 pistoles! Everything, in short, has its use,

A barbe de fol apprend-on à raire.

In Elizabeth's reign periwigs made their appearance, and were worn very generally by ladies of rank. Paul Hentzner, writing of the queen, then in her sixty-seventh year, says she wore false hair, and that red, with a small crown on her head. False hair of different colours was worn on different occasions by the same person: sometimes the queen appeared in black hair.

Mary Queen of Scots had black hair; but in some of her portraits she is represented with light hair, and, in accordance with the fashion of her day, she frequently wore borrowed locks of different colours. Knollys, in a letter to Cecil, makes mention of one "Mistress Mary Seaton, greatly praised by the queen, and one of the finest *buskers* to be seen in any country. Among other pretty devices, she did set a curled hair upon the queen that was said to be a *perewyke*, that showed very delicately; and every other day she hath a new device of head-dressing without any cost, and yet setteth forth a woman gayly well." Hair-powder first came into fashion in 1590.

Puttenham, in his "Art of Poesie," says, "Now again at this time the young gentlemen of the court *have taken up* the long haire trayling on their shoulders, and think this more decent, for what respect I should be glad to know." Curling the points of their beards and moustaches was a favourite style with the young men of fashion. The ladies wore the hair curled, frizzled, and crisped, and underpropped with pins and wires, and so tortured into the most fantastic shapes: we read, also, of cauls of hair set with seed-pearls and gold buttons.

In the days of our British Solomon there were first-rate coxcombs and exquisites; and some so solicitous about the beauty of the outward man, that, when they walked abroad, they carried a looking-glass "in a tobacco box or dial set." Towards the close of this reign, the hair of females was combed back in a roll over the forehead, and on this a small hood.

In France, when Louis XIII. came to the throne, he was too young to have a beard. For a time the beard was unfashionable; but whiskers were much in favour with gallants, and thought to be greatly admired by their lady-loves.

The peaked beard of Charles I., so well known from the portraits by Vandyke, introduces us to the troubled times of the Cavaliers and Roundheads. The aversion of the latter to the flowing curls of the Royalists was extreme, and led to the adoption of the Puritanical crop, which, as a mere negation and opposed to every principle of beauty, was doomed in turn to be discarded with ineffable contempt. One would wish to speak with all respect of the stout ironsides who fought at Marston Moor and Naseby; but the silly crusade, encouraged by some of the meaner sort against the beautiful creations of art, has done more to estrange men's minds from the noble principles they upheld with their swords, than the united acclaim of their preachers could effect in their behalf. The "*love-locks*" of the court gallants were especially hateful to the Puritans. Sometimes a single lock of hair, tied at the end with silk ribbon in bows, was allowed to fall on the chest; others wore two such love-locks, one on each side of the head, which, at times, reached to the waist. Prynne wrote a book expressly against them, on "The Unloveliness of Love-locks;" and in 1643 appeared Dr. Hall's tract "On the Loathsomeness of Long Hair," wherein he complained that "some have long lockes at their eares, as if they had four eares, or were prick-eared; some have a little long locke onely before, hanging down to their noses, like the taile of a weasall; every man being made a foole at the barber's pleasure, or making a foole of the barber for having to make him such a foole." And in Lyly's play of Midas, it is asked, "Will you have a low curl on your head, like a ball, or dangling locks, like a spaniel? Your moustachioes sharp at the ends, like a shoemaker's awl, or hanging down to your mouth, like goats' flakes? Your love-locks wreathed with a silken twist, or shaggy to fall on your shoulders?"

The reader cannot have failed to remark how these love-locks and periwigs facilitated the disguise of one sex for the other, so often assumed by characters in old plays, and on which the chief interest or plot of a piece frequently turned. Thus, when Julia, in "The Two Gentlemen of Verona," desires her maid, Lucetta, to provide her with "such weeds as may beseem some well-reputed page." Lucetta answers, "Why, then, your ladyship must cut your hair."

JULIA.—No, girl; I'll knit it up in silken strings,

With twenty odd conceited true-love knots:

To be fantastic, may become a youth

Of greater time than I shall show to be.

A periwig favored the escape of the Duke of York, afterwards James II., from St. James's Palace in 1648, who luckily "shifted into gentlewoman's clothes," got on board a Dutch vessel below Gravesend, and landed safely in Holland. The hostess at Middleburgh, where the prince slept by the way, wondered much that "the young gentlewoman would not let the maids help her to bed."

As a companion picture to the love locks of the gentlemen, the ladies adorned themselves with artificial ringlets, cunningly inserted amid the true; and *heart-breakers* (accroche-cœur), arranged with studied and most killing aim. The female coiffure of the Stuart period has always been much admired, with its soft clustering curls and semi-transparence, the effect of a peculiar friz. Some of the portraits of that era, the hair arranged with true feminine taste, gracefully shadowing a complexion of the utmost delicacy, are studies of female loveliness, which, once seen, are not easily forgotten.

Some years ago, the body of Charles the first was discovered at Windsor, and it is said the late Sir Henry Halford and George IV. were the only persons to whom it was shown. Sir Henry cut off a lock of the king's hair, and made Sir Walter Scott a present of a part, which he had set in virgin gold, the word "Remember" surrounding it in highly relieved letters.

Whiskers were still in fashion at the French court. The king, Turenne, Corneille, Moliere, and the chief men of note were proud to wear them. "It was then," says a grave encyclopedist, "no uncommon thing for a favourite lover to have his whiskers turned up, combed, and dressed by his mistress; and hence a man of fashion took care always to be provided with every little requisite, especially whisker-wax. It was highly flattering to a lady to have it in her power to praise the beauty of the lover's whiskers, which, far from being disgusting, gave his person an air of vivacity, and several even thought them an incitement to love." What would our gallant Drake have thought of this effeminacy, who, after he had burned Philip's fleet at Cadiz, in sailor's phrase called it "singeing the king of Spain's whiskers."

The Roundheads were mercilessly ridiculed in ballads, and pelted with poetry in every style of doggerel, till finally gibetted for the amusement of posterity by the author of Hudibras. The nick-name of Roundheads, we are told, arose from their putting a round bowl or wooden dish upon their heads, and cutting their hair by the edges or brim of the bowl. The bowl may, or may not, have been in use for this purpose, but nothing could exceed the ugliness of the Puritan crop.

"What creature's this, with his short hairs,

His little band, and huge long ears,

That a new faith has founded?"

Even such brave and noble-minded adherents as Colonel Hutchinson could not escape the censure of their own party for not conforming in all respects to the vulgar notions of orthodoxy. His long and beautiful hair was looked upon with suspicion as betraying a certain lukewarmness in their cause. The Puritans even forbade the women to wear braided hair. And some of them, more zealous than the rest, made a vow not to trim their beards till the parliament had subdued the king, as did Sir Hudibras.

'Twas to stand fast

As long as monarchy should last;

But when the state should hap to reel

'Twas to submit to fatal steel.

These vow-beards were also worn by some staunch old Jacobites, to mark their love for the house of Stuart, who hoped to see the king recalled to the throne. The beard of Sir Hudibras has acquired a sort of historical importance, and, to do it justice, must be pictured at full length:

"His tawny beard was th' equal grace

Both of his wisdom and his face;

In cut and die so like a tile,

A sudden view it would beguile;

The upper part whereof was whey,

The nether orange mix'd with grey.

This hairy meteor did denounce

The fall of sceptres and of crowns;

With grisly type did represent

Declining age of government,

And tell, with hieroglyphic spade,

Its own grave and the state's were made.

Like Samson's heart-breakers it grew,

In time to make a nation rue;

Though it contributed its own fall

To wait upon the public downfall."

What befel this tawny beard we learn from the same faithful narrative of the knight's adventures:

"At that an egg let fly,

Hit him directly o'er the eye,

And, running down his cheek, besmear'd

With orange tawny slime his beard;

But beard and slime being of one hue,

The wound the less appear'd to view."

In this terrible plight he is visited by the widow, one of Job's comforters, who begins her discourse with a commentary on beards, which must be our apology for inserting it here:

"If he that is in battle conquer'd

Have any title to his own beard,

Though yours be sorely lugg'd and torn,

It does your visage more adorn

Than if 'twere prun'd, and starch'd, and lander'd,

And cut square by the Russian standard."

Butler has left us a portrait of Philip Nye's Thanksgiving Beard, which must not be passed by unnoticed:

"This rev'rend brother, like a goat,

Did wear a tail upon his throat,

The fringe and tassel of a face,

That gives it a becoming grace;

But set in such a curious frame,

> As if 'twere wrought in filograin,
>
> And cut so e'en, as if't had been
>
> Drawn with a pen upon his chin:
>
> No topiary hedge of quickset,
>
> Was e'er so neatly cut, or thick-set."

It has been seriously asserted that paste-board cases were invented to put over these beards at night, lest their owners should turn upon and rumple them in their sleep. The Puritans carried their hatred of long hair with them to their new homes across the Atlantic. In a code of laws which they published, among other curious regulations it is set forth, "that it is a shameful practice for any man who has the least care for his soul to wear long hair. As this abomination excites the indignation of all pious persons, we, the magistrates, in our zeal for the purity of the faith, do expressly and authentically declare, that we condemn the impious custom of letting the hair grow—a custom which we look upon to be very indecent and dishonest, which terribly disguises men, and is offensive to modest and sober persons, inasmuch as it corrupts good manners," with much more to the like effect, in a strain of dreary verbiage and exhortation. Long hair, according to a Puritan poet, was nothing else than the banner of Satan displayed in triumph from a man's head.

Milton's beautiful hair, falling upon his shoulders in broad masses of clustering curls, and setting off features of rare beauty, is deserving of special honour. It is a question whether those sacred hairs were sacrilegiously handled by certain ruffianly overseers in 1790, during some repairs to the church of St. Giles, Cripplegate. If the body then exhumed, and presumed to be Milton's, were in reality the earthly remains of our great poet, these "sapient, trouble-tombs," after a carouse, (how wonderfully a parish feast smooths the way to some dirty job, so easily reconciled to the parochial mind), "cutting open the leaden coffin, found a body in its shroud, and, believing it to be that of the poet, they extracted the teeth, cut off the hair, which was six inches long, and combed and tied together, and then left the scattered remains to the grave diggers, who were permitted to exhibit them for money to the public. Mr. Philip Neve, of Furnival's Inn, who published an account of the transaction, was strongly convinced that the body was that of Milton, although the hair and other circumstances favoured the opinion that it was the body of a woman." Was anything more disgusting ever perpetrated in the days

> "When Bradshaw bullied in a broad-brimmed hat,"

or since?

The Restoration of Charles II. ushered in THE AGE OF GREAT WIGS—a subject of too much importance to be summarily disposed of, and which we purposely reserve for the next chapter.

WIGS.

CHAPTER IV

The introduction of the ample perriwig has always been regarded as the most ambitious effort of tonsorial art. And as it rarely happens that any one mind is capable of perfecting a discovery by a single effort; so the honour of conceiving the beau ideal of a fully-developed wig can scarcely, with justice, be claimed by any particular artist. Like the Absolutism, of which it may be regarded as the symbol, it was the growth of time, and expanded to its fullest dimensions under the favouring rule of the Grand Monarque. During that long reign, extending over the greater part of a century, the Wig sat supreme upon the brows of one of the great Princes of the Earth, at whose nod the nations trembled; whose wrath was fire and desolation, as the ruined towns of the Palatinate may still bear witness (Rex dixit, et factum est); whose ambition was fed with war and conquest; but whose heart was all as false as the smooth curls which counterfeited the graces of perpetual youth.

The true morphological development of the wig appears to have been after this fashion. First of all a small portion of artificial hair was cunningly inserted among the natural curls, to eke out the economy of Nature; this suggested the idea of two supplementary bunches; then a third was added; these in turn were connected by a coif, and the result was the *perruque à calotte*. It is recorded of the Cardinal de Richelieu that he was the first to introduce this form of peruke at court. It formed part of the attire of the Duke of Bedford, so whimsically described by De Grammont to Charles II. "Sir," said he, "I had the honour to see him embark in his coach, with his asthma, and country equipage, his *perruque à calotte* neatly tied with a yellow riband, and his old-fashioned hat covered with oil-skin, which became him uncommonly well." The first appearance of Louis Quatorze in his grand peruke is not duly set forth with historic accuracy; but the important part it played in the daily routine of court etiquette is well known. The chief valet slept in the king's apartment and called him at the appointed hour. Then it was announced in the ante-chamber that the king was awake. In came the members of the royal family to wish him "good morning;" after them, the first gentleman of the chamber, the grand master of the wardrobe and other officers bringing the king's dresses. From a silver gilt vessel the valet pours spirits of wine on the royal hands, and a duke presents the holy water. After a very short religious service, the king's perruques are laid before him, and choice is made of one most pleasing to his majesty, which is subsequently elevated to the head by the king's own hand. Other ceremonies disposed of, the king must be shaved: one holds the basin, another adjusts the shaving-cloth and applies the razor; a soft sponge dipped in spirit of wine is passed over the royal face, and afterwards pure water in the same manner, which completes the operation, the chief valet all the time holding the looking-glass. At all the mysteries of *la première entrée*, the *grand entrée*, and the dressing of the king by the courtiers, the ceremony of the breakfast, and the state receptions, the peruke is present. But before proceeding to the council, the chief valet furnishes another wig for the king's pate: it goes to mass with him, attends him at dinner, accompanies him to the abode of Madame de Maintenon and elsewhere; comes home in good time, and is present at the supper *au grand couvert*: then bows to the ladies and courtiers in the grand saloon, and returns with the king for a while to his own apartments to witness the felicities of a king in private life. About midnight again all is bustle and preparation; the chief barber arranges the dressing table in the king's chamber; a cold collation is put by the bedside, ready to the king's lips, should he wake with an appetite in the night; the courtiers are assembled, and the king enters. He hands his hat and gloves to some favoured nobleman who is present to receive them, the sword by knightly hands is carried to the dressing-table, the almoner holds the wax lights and repeats the prayer, the watch and reliquary are given in charge to a valet de chambre, blue ribbon, cravat and waistcoat are dispensed with, two lacqueys remove the garters, two more are required to draw off the stockings, two pages present slippers, and the Dauphin the *chemise de nuit*; the king bows, the courtiers retire, and the *grand coucher* is finished. Now the hair has to be combed and arranged; one valet holds the looking-glass and the other a light; the bed is aired, and the Wig goes to bed with the king; the chief valet draws the curtains, and, within the secret recesses of that impenetrable shade, the perriwig is exchanged for a nightcap, and the royal hand of Louis presenting it outside the curtains, it is consigned to the care of its trusty guardian, the chief valet, who then locks the doors, and lays down on a bed prepared for him in the same chamber. Good night, Monsieur Bontemps.—What if some of these wonderful wigs could publish their "Secret Memoirs," what a treasury of scandal it would disclose for the gratification of the pickers-up of "unconsidered trifles!"

Binette was the great perruquier of that Augustan age. Without his aid neither king nor courtiers could go forth in becoming fashion. His carriage and running footmen were constantly to be seen passing to and fro the streets of Paris, in attendance on the nobility. In 1656, Louis le Grand appointed forty wig-makers to wait upon the Court, and in 1673 a corporation of *Barbiers-perruquiers*, consisting of 200 members, was established to supply the commonalty of Paris. At one time the minister Colbert, judging from the large sum of money remitted from France to foreign countries for hair, that the balance of trade was against his own country, was desirous of introducing some kind of cap to take the place of the wig, and spoke to the king on the subject; but the wig-makers took the alarm, memorialized the king, and showed from statistics that the profit on wigs exported from Paris more than equalled the sum paid to foreigners for the material; so that Colbert's project was laid aside, and wigs and wig-makers flourished more than ever. The number of licenses was now increased to 850, and the members known under the title of *barbiers-perruquiers, baigneurs-etuvistes.* The corporation had its provost, wardens, and syndics, which were appointed by letters patent, and the offices were hereditary. The king bestowed on this corporation the sole right of dealing in hair, either by wholesale or retail; of making and selling powder or pomatum; preparations to remove the hair; drops for the cure of toothache, &c. The use of powder was not at first sanctioned by the monarch, but at last he yielded to the wishes of his courtiers, and permitted a trifling quantity to be sprinkled on his own perukes. Not only was the wig a thing of magnitude, it possessed also considerable weight; a stylish wig weighed rather more than a couple of pounds, and was worth, according to the best authorities, a thousand crowns. Light hair was most esteemed, and fetched at times as much as eighty francs the ounce. To prevent imposition, it was ordered that no second-hand wigs should be sold, except by certain dealers on the *Quai de l'Horloge.* When these costly wigs were first introduced the wearers appeared in the streets, in all sorts of weather, with their hats in their hands, so anxious were they not to disarrange their well-ordered curls. Menage has preserved a poem of that period which ridicules the custom, and concludes thus:

> "Critics, how narrow are your views,
>
> Who thus the prudent youth abuse!
>
> By a just value he is led
>
> Both of his wig and of his head;
>
> The one he knows was dearly bought,
>
> The other would not fetch a groat."

Bernini, the sculptor, once ventured to arrange the monarch's curls in accordance with his own notions of classic dignity. He had been sent for, from Rome, at great expense, to superintend some additions to the Louvre, and was engaged on a bust of Louis, when perceiving that the king's forehead was too much over-shadowed with curls, he thrust them back, saying to the king, "Your Majesty's face should be seen by every one." This originated the *frisure à la Bernin.*

Combing these elaborate curls was the envied occupation of the beaux. In that inimitable dramatic sketch by Molière, "Les Précieuses Ridicules," which resembles a clever etching by a master-hand, it will be remembered that Mascarille, the pretended marquis, combs his curls in the presence of the ladies with the usual blandishments. The scented powder with which these wigs were besprinkled was selected with the nicest judgment and at great cost. In this respect also, Mascarille, who had made free with his master's clothes, the better to make love in the court fashion to the fair *precieuse*, was as well furnished as any of the court gallants.

Mascarille.

Et celle-la? (Il donne à sentir les cheveux poudrés de sa perruque.)

Madelon.

Elle est tout à fait de qualité; le sublime en est touché délicieusement.

Well might Gorgibus, in choleric mood exclaim:

Ces pendardes-là, avec leur pommade, ont, je pense, envie de me ruiner. Je ne vois partout que blancs d'œufs, lait virginal, et mille autres brimborions que je ne connais point. Elles ont usé, depuis que nous sommes ici, le lard d'une douzaine de couchons, pour le moins; et quatre valets vivraient tous les jours des pieds de moutons qu'elles emploient.

We are not well enough informed in such manners to know if these family recipes be worthy to be compared with the "capons greaz" which good Queen Bess carried with her, as we learn from Nichol's "Progresses," to make the hair to shine like a mallard's wing. We own to a natural dread of such domestic manufactures, and always greatly admired that fine piece of strategy on the part of Dr. Primrose, when observing his daughters busily concocting some compound over the fire—and informed by little Dick of its true nature—he grases the poker and capsizes the ingredients.

The nomenclature of wigs is very ample, a complete system of classification might be adopted, and genus and species discriminated with the greatest nicety; there were Wigs Military, Legal, Ecclesiastical, and Infantile; we can only find room for a few varieties:

- Perruque à bonnet.
- —— à nœuds.
- —— ronde.
- —— pointue.
- —— naissante.
- —— à deux queues.
- —— à tonsure.
- —— à la brigadière.

- —— de l'Abbé.

- —— à boudin.

- —— à papillons.

- —— à deux marteaux.

- —— à trois marteaux.

- —— à bourse.

We shall only be following the usual course of Fashion if we pass from the French Court to Whitehall. In England the ladies are said to have been beforehand with the gentlemen in the great Wig movement. Pepys writes (1662), "By and bye came La Belle Pierce to see my wife, and to bring her a pair of perruques of hair as the fashion now is for ladies to wear, which are pretty, and one of my wife's own hair, or else I should not endure them." The year following Pepys made a similar investment on his own account— "November 3, Home, and by and bye comes Chapman, the perriwig maker, and upon my liking it (the wig), without more ado, I went up, and then he cut off my haire, which went a little to my heart at present to part with it; but it being over, and my perriwig on, I paid him £3, and away went he with my own haire to make up another of; and I by and bye went abroad, after I had caused all my maids to look upon it, and they concluded it do become me, though Jane was mightily troubled for my parting with my own hair, and so was Besse.

"November 8, Lord's Day.—To church, where I found that my coming in a perriwig did not prove so strange as I was afraid it would, for I thought that all the church would presently have cast their eyes on me, but I found no such things."

The same minute chronicler informs us that the Duke of York put on a perriwig in February, 1663, and that he saw the king in one for the first time the following April.

By command of Charles II., members of the University of Cambridge were forbidden to wear perriwigs; and, on another occasion, when a chaplain was preaching before him in a wig, he bid the Duke of Monmouth, then chancellor of the university, to cause the statutes concerning decency of apparel to be more strictly enforced. To be deprived of their wigs was a clerical grievance. In France, a turbulent priest at the cathedral of Beauvais insisted on his right to wear one at mass, but was hindered from doing so, when he solemnly placed the objectionable wig in the hands of a notary at the church doors, and protested against the indignity which had been put upon him.

The year of the Great Plague was one of the most terrible in our annals—Death smote his victims by thousands—the voice of lamentation and mourning stilled for a time the gaieties of a dissolute court. The men of fashion became alarmed lest the poison of the plague might lurk insidiously in the curls of their wigs. Pepys entertained the same fear:—"September 3, (1664).—Up, and put on my coloured silk suit, very fine, and my new perriwig, bought a good while since, but durst not wear, because the plague was in Westminster when I bought it; and it is a wonder what will be the fashion after the plague is done as to perriwigs, for nobody will buy any hair for fear of infection, that it had been cut off the heads of people dead of the plague."

Wigs were first worn by barristers about 1670. The judges were at first somewhat opposed to the innovation, as suited only to fops, and unbecoming so learned a profession; and some of the more zealous leaders of the fashion were not suffered to plead in their new attire. Time has long since reconciled us to the forensic head-dress; and if the public be at all sceptical as to the merits of horse-hair, the rare talents it has fostered would alone command respect. Custom and precedent have now securely enthroned the wig in the Halls of Justice, and authority looks with suspicion on any attempt to interfere with its prerogative. Lord Campbell tells us that when he argued the great Privilege Case, and had to speak for sixteen hours, "he obtained leave to speak without a wig; but under the condition that it was not to be drawn into a precedent."

As early as 1654, Evelyn had been shocked at the discovery that ladies of fashion painted their cheeks; and Pepys records that in the galleries at Whitehall he beheld the ladies of honour "just for all the world like men with doublets buttoned up to the breast, and with perriwigs and hats." How closely French fashions were imitated at Whitehall we may judge from an entry in Evelyn's diary:—"Following his majesty this morning through the gallery, I went with the few who attended him into the Duchess of Portsmouth's dressing-room, where she was in her morning loose garment, her maids combing her, newly out of her bed, his majesty and the gallants standing about her." Although modesty, which ever accompanies good taste, had fled the court of Charles, some fine examples might be selected from the Court Beauties, as illustrating the special beauty of a natural and becoming coiffure. De Grammont has not failed to notice the hair of La Belle Hamilton, which was well set, and fell with ease into that natural order which is so difficult to imitate. Miss Jenning's hair was of a most beauteous flaxen, adorning the brightest complexion that ever was seen. And the portraits of Nell Gwynn show that sprightly damsel with short ringlets about the temples, massed like bunches of grapes, in most tempting clusters.

Among the smaller works of art which the perruquier produced for the fair sex, we may mention a description of false hair set on wires, so as to stand out like wings from each side of the head; and the merkin, so called, which was arranged in a group of curls at each side of the face, small over the forehead and thence increasing like the lower part of a pyramid.

During the brief reign of James II. wigs grew larger still, and false hair put the natural ornament of a man's head completely in the shade. Holme, writing in 1688, assures his readers that the custom of wearing wigs, then so much used by the generality of men, "was quite contrary to the custom of their forefathers, who got estates, loved their wives, and wore their own hair," and adds pathetically, "in these days there be no such things." The love-lock was soon engrafted on the wig, to which allusion is made in Beaumont and Fletcher's "Cupid's Revenge:"

> "He lay in gloves all night, and this morning I
>
> Brought him a new perriwig with a lock at it."

There was, also, a long perriwig in vogue with a pole-lock or *suffloplin*, as the perruquiers termed it, the prototype of the giant pig-tails, once so dear to the army and navy, who never turn tail on the enemy. We read, likewise, of the travelling or campaign-wig, with long knots or twisted tails tied with ribbon, depending from the bottom of the wig laterally—technically styled "knots or bobs, or a dildo on each side with a curled forehead."

In the next reign wigs still went on increasing in size. Combing the curls in public, or when flirting with the ladies, was esteemed *haut ton*. Ivory or tortoiseshell combs of large size were carried in the gentlemen's pockets, with which they imitated Mascarille, we make no doubt, very abominably. They certainly manage these things much better in France: in fashion we are content to be servile imitators of the French, and the copy is usually very inferior to the original. Madame Sevigné, in one of her charming letters, gossiping about the Duchess de Bourbon, writes:—"Rien n'est plus plaisant que d'assister à sa toilette, et de la voir se coiffer; j'y fus l'autre jour: elle s'éveilla à midi et demi, prit sa robe de chambre, vint se coiffer, et manger un pain au pot; elle se frise et se poudre elle-même, elle mange en même tems; les mêmes doigts tiennent alternativement la houppe et le pain au pot; elle mange sa poudre et graisse ses cheveux; le tout ensemble fait un fort bon déjeuné et une charmante coiffure." To this age belongs the extraordinary head-dress usually called a commode: the hair was combed upwards from off the forehead, and upon this was built a huge pile of ribbons and lace, arranged in tiers, and over all a scarf or veil drooping on the neck and shoulders. It rivalled the fabled turrets which crown the head of Cybele, and was worn by Queen Mary herself as part of the court costume. In England these were Halcyon days for wig-makers. In later years wigs were more generally worn by all classes; but, for the most part, they were wigs for the million, more moderate in their pretensions, till at last they dwindled down to a mere apology for a wig. The quantity of hair alone in a wig for a nobleman or gentleman in those high and palmy days of wig-making was more than ten natural crops could furnish. The material was most costly. In 1700, a young country girl received £60 for her head of hair; and the grey locks of an old woman, after death, sold for fifty pounds: the ordinary price of a wig was about forty pounds. Full-bottomed wigs, invented by one Duviller, to conceal, it is said, a want of symmetry in the shoulders of the Dauphin, were appropriated by the learned professions and those who studied to look uncommonly grave and sagacious.

> "Physic of old her entry made
>
> Beneath the immense full-bottom's shade,
>
> While the gilt cane, with solemn pride,
>
> To each sagacious nose applied,
>
> Seemed but a necessary prop
>
> To bear the weight of wig at top."

Children, too, wore wigs; and, if unprovided with so necessary an article of dress, the hair was combed and curled, so as to look as much like a wig as possible.

Archbishop Tillotson was the first of our prelates who wore a wig. In one of his sermons he writes: "I can remember when ministers generally, whatever their text was, did either find or make occasion to reprove the sin of long hair; and if they saw any one in the congregation guilty in that kind, they would point him out particularly, and let fly at him with great zeal."

The reign of Queen Anne saw the magnitude of the wig somewhat diminished, but the variety of wigs in fashion was increased. Steele's wig at one time formed a heavy item in his expenditure. His large black perriwig cost him (we are supposing it was paid for) as much as forty guineas. Swift had a fine state wig for grand occasions waiting his coming to St. James's, as did poor Vanessa. Colley Cibber's wig, in which he played a favourite character, was of such noble proportions, that it was brought upon the stage in a sedan by two chairmen. How it was that Colonel Brett desired to possess this formidable wig, at any price, must be told in Cibber's own words: "Possibly, the charms of our theatrical nymphs might have had some share in drawing him thither; yet, in my observation, the most visible cause of his first coming was a more sincere passion he had conceived for a fair full-bottom'd perriwig, which I then wore in my first play of the *Fool in Fashion*. * * * Now, whatever contempt philosophers may have for a fine perriwig, my friend, who was not to despise the world, but to live in it, knew very well that so material an article of dress upon the head of a man of sense, if it became him, could never fail of drawing to him a more partial regard and benevolence than could possibly be hoped for in an ill-made one,—terms were offered—and it ended in an agreement to finish our bargain that night over a bottle." "That single bottle was the sire of many a jolly dozen," at their subsequent meetings, as he explains further on.

The tie-wig, an abridgment of the long curled perriwig, was worn by many, but was not considered court dress. Lord Bolingbroke, having to wait upon the queen in haste, once went to court in a tie-wig, which so offended Queen Anne, that she said to those about her, "I suppose his lordship will come to court the next time in a nightcap." Swift writes, (1712): "As prince Eugene was going with Mr. Secretary to court, Mr. Hoffman, the Emperor's resident, said to his highness that it was not proper to go to court without a long wig, and his was a tied up one. "Now," says the prince, "I know not what to do, for I never had a long perriwig in my life; and I have sent to all my valets and footmen, to see whether any of them had one, that I might borrow it; but none of them had any." But the secretary said "was a thing of no consequence, and only observed by gentlemen ushers." After the battle of Ramillies, the name of the Ramillie-wig was given to a wig with a long tapering tail, plaited and tied, with a great bow at the top, and a smaller one at the bottom."

The little incident of Lord Petre depriving Mrs. Fermor of a ringlet gave rise to Pope's poem "The Rape of the Lock." Belinda's head-dress is thus described:

> "This nymph, to the destruction of mankind,
>
> Nourished two locks, which graceful hung behind
>
> In equal curls, and well conspired to deck
>
> With shining ringlets the smooth ivory neck.
>
> Love in these labyrinths his slaves detains,
>
> And mighty hearts are held in slender chains."

The poet explains how these "mazy ringlets," owed much of their beauty to a rigorous discipline:

> "Was it for this you took such constant care
>
> The bodkin, comb, and essence to prepare?
>
> For this your locks in paper durance bound,
>
> For this with torturing irons wreathed around?
>
> For this with fillets strained your tender head,
>
> And bravely bore the double loads of lead?"

Belinda's lock, in imitation of the lost tresses of Berenice, is translated to the heavenly regions:

> "A sudden star, it shot through liquid air,
>
> And drew behind a radiant trail of hair."

A compliment to Belinda appropriately concludes the poem:

> "When these fair suns shall set, as set they must,
>
> And all those tresses shall be laid in dust,
>
> This lock the Muse shall consecrate to fame,
>
> And 'midst the stars inscribe Belinda's name."

In Swift's verses called "Death and Daphne," we have a metaphorical description of a beau's wig:

> "From her own head Megara takes
>
> A perriwig of twisted snakes,
>
> Which in the nicest fashion curl'd,
>
> (Like toupées of this upper world),
>
> With flour of sulphur powder'd well,
>
> That graceful on his shoulders fell.
>
> An adder of the sable kind
>
> In line direct hung down behind."

Both old and young fops carried the follies of the wig mania to a most ridiculous extent. The author of the "London Spy" introduces us to a smart young fellow "with a wheelbarrow full of perriwig on;" and that impudent fellow, Tom Brown, in his "Letters from the Dead to the Living," writing of a certain beau, styled Beau Whittaker, says, "His perriwig was large enough to have loaded a camel, and he had bestowed upon it at least a bushel of powder;" and speaking elsewhere of another fop, with a perriwig of the same dimensions, he observes, "If Nature had indulged our primitive parents with such an extraordinary production, they would have had little reason to have blushed at, or been ashamed of their nakedness." To speak seriously, if the wig did not quite clothe the body like a tunic, it more than concealed the head. The malicious spy we have quoted above comes across another fopling in a fine wig, and moralizes after this manner: "His head is a fool's egg hid in a nest of hair." If we accompany him to Man's Coffee House, we shall see, "a gaudy crowd of *Tom Essences* walking backwards and forwards with their hats in their hands, not daring to convert them to their intended use, lest it should put the foretops of their wigs into some disorder; their whole exercise being to charge and discharge their nostrils, and keep their perriwigs in proper order." The fortune of a life not unfrequently turned upon the imposing—we should have said the captivating appearance of a wig: unluckily in every lottery there are many blanks; and Addison tells of one inveterate fortune-hunter, who "had combed and powdered at the ladies for thirty years."

There were some inconveniences attending the use of wigs. There was no such thing as walking forth to enjoy fresh air and exercise except in the finest weather, if attired as became a gentleman; to be carried about by chairmen, and jolted in a sort of trunk or band-box was a most unenviable distinction. If a dark cloud hung over the Park or the Mall, away hurried the magnificent perriwigs—away flew the pretty women in their hoods and ribbons. Gay, in his "Trivia," sounds the note of warning:

> "When suffocating mists obscure the morn,
>
> Let the worst wig, long used to storms be worn;
>
> This knows the powdered footman, and with care
>
> Beneath his flapping hat secures his hair.
>
> *   *   *   in vain you scow'r
>
> Thy wig alas! uncurl'd, admits the show'r.
>
> So fierce Alecto's snaky tresses fell,
>
> When Orpheus charm'd the vig'rous powers of hell
>
> Or thus hung Glaucus beard, with briny dew

Clotted and straight, when first his am'rous view

Surprised the bathing fair."

Swift, in the "City Shower," laughs at the distressed wigs:

"Here various kinds, by various fortunes led Commence acquaintance underneath a shed. Triumphant Tories and desponding Whigs Forget their feuds, and join to save their wigs."

To be caught in the rain was a terrible ordeal for the curls; but accidents by fire were still more calamitous. At a display of fireworks, an old writer says, the spectators screwed themselves up in the balconies to avoid the fireworks, "which instantly assaulted the perukes of the gallants and the merkins of the madams." Wigs, too, being of considerable value, were frequently stolen from the head. Gay gives an instance of a very artful dodge:

"Where the mob gathers swiftly shoot along,

Nor idly mingle in the noisy throng.

*****

Nor is thy flaxen wig with safety worn.

High on the shoulder, in the basket borne,

Lurks the sly boy, whose hand to rapine bred,

Plucks off the curling honours of the head."

To be brought into actual contact with a powdered beau, was reckoned one of the misadventures which a prudent man would wish to avoid.

"You'll sometimes meet a fop of nicest tread,

Whose mantling peruke veils his empty head,

At every step he dreads the wall to lose,

And risks, to save a coach, his red-heeled shoes;

Him, like the miller, pass with caution by,

Lest from his shoulders clouds of powder fly."

While the coarser sex revelled in all the luxury of full perriwigs, we may be sure the fair sex bestowed as great attention on their hair. If enterprises of great moment were undertaken by the wigs, there was fearful slaughter of human hearts from the masked batteries of the ladies' smiles. In "Love's Bill of Mortality," given at length in the *Spectator*, we read of one, "Jack Freelove, murdered by Melissa in her hair."

"The toilet," says Addison, "is their great scene of business, and the right adjustment of their hair the principal employment of their lives."

> "At her toilet she puts on every toy
>
> That ladies use when eager to destroy;
>
> Three hours by the clock, (and some say four),
>
> She sat in polishing her form all o'er,
>
> And culling arrows from her fatal store."

The resources of a lady's toilet were too numerous to be brought within the compass of Cowley's verse. He declines

> "To relate
>
> The strength and riches of their state—
>
> The powder, patches, and the pins,
>
> The ribbons, jewels, and the rings,
>
> The lace, the paint, and warlike things,
>
> That make up all their magazines."

And, fortunately, what he despaired of accomplishing lies beyond the limits of our present subject. But the time spent at the toilet was not all dedicated to dress and the tire-woman. Addison's skilful pen will supply an apt illustration; "Sempronia is at present the most professed admirer of the French nation; but is so modest as to admit her visitants no farther than her toilet. It is a very odd sight that beautiful creature makes when she is talking politics, with her tresses flowing about her shoulders, and examining that face in the glass, which does such execution upon the standers-by. How prettily does she divide her discourse between her woman and her visitants! What sprightly transitions does she make from an opera or a sermon to an ivory comb or a pin-cushion! How have I been pleased to see her interrupted in an account of her travels by a message to her footman, and holding her tongue in the midst of a moral reflection by applying the tip of it to a patch!"

> "Vanessa held Montaigne and read,
>
> Whilst Mrs. Susan combed her head,"

The Duchess of Sunderland, daughter of the celebrated Duchess of Marlborough, and like her mother, says Horace Walpole, conspicuous for her long and beautiful hair; was a great politician, and used, when combing it, to receive the visits of those whose vote and interest she sought to influence. While Queen Anne dressed, prayers used to be read in an outer room, and once ordering the door to be shut while she shifted, the chaplain stopped. The queen sent to ask why he did not proceed. He replied, "He would not whistle the word of God through the key-hole." The author of the "Reminiscences" adds, that Queen Caroline was wont to dispatch her toilet and hear prayers in the same fashion. The Duchess of Marlborough on one occasion was somewhat prodigal of her fine fair hair, of which she had the greatest abundance; for being engaged at her toilet, in a fit of anger towards the Duke, she cut off those commanding tresses and flung them in his face.

The beauties of those days made politics, the card table, and the toilet, their chief study, and

> "Thought the life of ev'ry lady
>
> Should be one continued play-day—
>
> Balls, and masquerades, and shows,
>
> Visits, plays, and powdered beaus."

The wits and poets of that brilliant era, have hit off the manners of the times, and all the paraphernalia of patches, fans, hoops, and head-dresses, by a few touches of the pen, with such airy grace and lightness in the true spirit of comic revelry, and with keenest irony, that more modern efforts in the same style appear, by comparison, coarse and clumsy. In our own day one would think the artists all copied from the same model,

> "Small waist, wide flounces, and a face divine,
>
> Wretchedly foolish, and extremely fine."

The ladies' head-dresses, which, in the time of William III., had shot up to a height which would have astonished even De Grammont's Princess of Babylon, had now fallen many degrees. Addison remarks, "some ten years ago, the female part of our species were much taller than the men. The women were of such an enormous stature, "that we appeared as grasshoppers before them." At present the whole sex is in a manner dwarfed and shrunk into a race of beauties that seems almost another species. I remember several ladies who were very near seven feet high that at present want some inches of five. How they came to be thus curtailed I could never learn:"

> Instead of home-spun coifs were seen
>
> Good pinners edged with Colberteen.

Old ladies continued for some time longer to adhere to the huge head-dresses, which supplied Lady Wortley Montague with a bit of raillery for her "Town Eclogues:"

> At chapel shall I wear the morn away?
>
> Who there appears at these unmodish hours
>
> But ancient matrons with their frizzled towers.

Queen Anne in the latter years of her reign wore her hair in a simple, graceful style, well suited to her quiet nature, with clusters of curls at the back of the neck; nor was any hair-powder permitted to sully the brightness of her chesnut ringlets. Her sweet voice seems still to plead for her with posterity, and to be remembered with something like affection, when the splendid victories of the great Marlborough are losing somewhat of their lustre on the page of history. The fruits of industry and the blessings of peace are too precious to be weighed against the glories of war. But, who can look at the portraits of Marlborough, with the long curls of the wig resting on the cuirass, without feeling there was truth in the saying of a foreigner, "That his looks were full as conquering as his sword."

How to wear a wig was part of the education of a man of the world, not to be learned from books. Those who know what witchcraft there is in the handling of a fan, what dexterity in the "nice conduct of a clouded cane," will imagine the wits and gentlemen of old did not suffer the wig to overshadow their temples with perpetual gloom, like the wreath of smoke which overhangs our Modern Babylon. And many a country squire must have tried in vain to catch the right toss of the head; to sport a playful humour in those crisp curls; or to acquire the lofty carriage of the foretop, or the significant trifling with some obtrusive lock; and felt as awkward in his new wig as a tailor on horseback, or a fat alderman with a dress sword dangling between his legs. There must have been something truly ridiculous in the prostrations of the perriwig-pated fop, who

> Returns the diving bow he did adore,
>
> Which with a shag casts all the hair before,

Till he with full decorum brings it back,

And rises with a water-spaniel shake.

For many years wigs were worn of the natural colour of the hair, but about 1714 it became customary to have them bleached; this, however, was not found to answer, as they soon turned of a disagreeable shade, so that recourse was had to hair-powder, the use of which soon became general. At the accession of George 1st, it is mentioned that only two ladies wore hair-powder. White perukes were characteristic of the early Georgian era. About the same period we notice that one side only of the wig was frequently tied together into a sort of club which hung down upon the chest in a very lop-sided fashion. A few years later bag-wigs were in vogue; when first introduced in France they were only worn *en déshabille*; in a short time, however, they came to be regarded as the most essential part of the full-dress costume of a beau. The French bag-wig, as it was styled, when it first made its appearance among us, was called in ridicule a fan-tail, and said to resemble the winged cap of Mercury; the women likened the bag-wigs to asses' ears, and the men retorted by allusion to the horns which were visible in a lady's head-gear. The *tu quoque* has ever been the ready argument with both sexes.

Follies they have so numberless the store,

That only we who love them can have more.

In some satirical verses, published 1753, the contour of the wig, set off from the face, is clearly shown:

"Let a well-frizzled wig be set off from his face;

With a bag quite in taste, from Paris just come,

That was made and tied up by Monsieur Frisson;

With powder quite grey—then his head is complete;—"

The tie-wig, which Lord Bolingbroke helped to bring into fashion, was a very stiff and solid affair, as compared with the long curled perriwigs which preceded them. The curls appear as if hardened into rollers; and the pendant lumps of hair, looped and tied at the ends, as if modelled after the fashion of the proud horse-tails, turned up and bound with straw, at a fair. It would be as difficult to determine why such cumbrous wigs were tolerated without any beauty to recommend them, as to say why George I. chose such ugly German mistresses. Was it because, like certain kinds of old china, deformity was pleasing? The king's favourites might possibly resemble the china, but the wigs were certainly not as frail. Horace Walpole has left us a lively description of Lord Sandwich's tie-wig, in a letter to Sir H. Mann, 1745: "I would speak to our new ally, and your old acquaintance, Lord Sandwich, to assist in it; but I could have no hope of getting at his ear, for he has put on such a first-rate tie-wig, on his admission to the admiralty-board, that nothing without the lungs of a boatswain can ever think to penetrate the thickness of the curls. I think, however, it does honour to the dignity of ministers: when he was but a patriot, his wig was not of half its present gravity." We have yet to notice the wig with the long *queue*, "small by degrees and beautifully less"—the drollest and most awkward of all additions to the human form since the long tails in Kent were inflicted on the men by a miracle, as a punishment for sticking fish tails to some monks' garments.

"As I live!

The hair of one is tied behind,

And plaited like a womankind,

While t'other carries on his back,

In silken bag, a monstrous pack:

But pray, what's that much like a whip,

Which with the air does waving skip

From side to side, and hip to hip?

It is a modish pig-tail wig."

When the Czar Peter was in Holland he made free with a burgomaster's wig in a very characteristic manner. He was at church: the service was somewhat dull, and his head getting cold, when, observing a good warm wig on the head of a fat functionary near him, he clapped it on his own pate, and did not restore it until the service was over. Churchill, the poet, used to declare that his career at Oxford was cut short by a large bushy wig, which added such a sage solemnity to the grave aspect of the examiner's face, that he could not control his laughter. Churchill had his jest, and was rejected at the examination. Garrick himself was once driven from the stage by a fit of laughter, brought on at the sight of a powdered wig. A Whitechapel butcher in a church-warden's wig, accompanied by his dog, occupied seats in front of the stage. Garrick was playing Lear, and preparing for a triumph at the end of the fifth act. The butcher, overcome with heat and mental excitement, was in a melting mood; to relieve which, he took off his wig, and placed it on the dog's head, who advanced to the orchestra, holding himself up by the fore-paws. At the critical moment, when inspiration seemed to animate every tone and gesture of the great actor, it chanced that his eye, "in a fine frenzy rolling," lighted on his four legged critic, who was as intent as any biped present on the scene before him, and quite indifferent to his large well-powdered Sunday peruke. At the moment the effect was irresistible; the dog outdid Garrick, who fairly ran off the stage amid roars of laughter from the whole house.

Of old, the doctor who set up in business without a wig in the best style of art was as little likely to succeed in his profession as a modern physician without his carriage.

> "Each son of Sol, to make him look more big,
>
> Had on a large, grave, decent, three tailed wig."

Of course, we don't suppose that Dr. Brocklesby's barber or the learned doctor intended it as an advertisement; but it was the constant practice of his barber to carry the said doctor's wig in its box through the crowd at the Exchange, calling out, "Make way for Dr. Brocklesby's wig!" Our allusion is to the dignity and importance of the wig, which were fully recognized by the honourable and illustrious professors of the healing art, who will please to excuse our indulging in a pleasant stave of an old song:

> "If you would see a noble wig,
>
> And in that wig a man look big,
>
> To Ludgate-hill repair, my joy,
>
> And gaze on Doctor Delmayhoy."

The parson was as well found in wigs as the doctor. Mandeville says of a wealthy parson, "His wigs are as fashionable as that form he is forced to comply with will admit of; but, as he is only stinted in their shape, so he takes care that for goodness of hair and colour few noblemen shall be able to match 'em." It is encouraging to know that the clergy look so closely to the goodness of the article they put before us. Warton wrote an "Ode to a Grizzle Wig," which is not the worst ingredient in that pleasant miscellany of his, "The Oxford Sausage:"

> "All hail, ye *Curls*, that rang'd in rev'rend row,
>
> With snowy pomp my conscious shoulders hide!
>
> That fall beneath in venerable flow,
>
> And crown my brows above with feathery pride!

High on your summit, wisdom's mimick'd air

    Sits thron'd with pedantry, her solemn sire,

And in her net of awe-diffusing hair,

    Entangles fools, and bids the crowd admire.

O'er every lock, that floats in full display,

    Sage ignorance her gloom scholastic throws;

And stamps o'er all my visage, once so gay,

    Unmeaning gravity's serene repose.

      *****

But thou, farewell, my *Bob*! whose thin wove thatch

    Was stor'd with quips and cranks, and wanton wiles,

That love to live within the *one-curled scratch*,

    With fun and all the family of smiles.

      *****

No more the wherry feels my stroke so true;

    At skittles in a *grizzle*, can I play?

Woodstock, farewell! and Wallingford adieu!

    Where many a scheme relieved the lingering day.

Such were the joys that once HILARIO crown'd,

    Ere grave preferment came my peace to rob;

Such are the less ambitious pleasures found

    Beneath the *liceat* of an humble *Bob*."

But at Bath the clergy thought of other things beside divinity lectures and professorships. Anstey tells of a young spark of a clergyman sporting about in a more fashionable, but less canonical, coiffure than the grizzle-wig:

    "What a cropt head of hair the young parson has on

    Emerged from his grizzle, the unfortunate sprig

Seems as if he were hunting all night for his wig."

Lely and Kneller could best illustrate the heroic age of wigs; but Hogarth's ready pencil furnishes abundant details of their social state. The comic element seems to abound in all his sketches of wigs. In his print of "The Bench," they slumber in the softest repose, in undisturbed gravity, and nod with the profoundest humour. The eminent lawyers were not all senior wranglers in those days. Look at the print of "The Country Dance," and say if ever wigs hung more unbecomingly on the shoulders of the most awkward frights; but for an enormous pig-tail wig where could we select a finer specimen than in the print of "Taste in High Life." These choice Exotics, as he has labelled them, are evidently great favourites with this humourous artist. But the print we are most concerned with is "THE FIVE ORDERS OF PERIWIGS, *as they were worn at the late Coronation, measured Architectonically.*" At the foot of the print the following advertisement is added:

In about 17 years will be completed, in 6 vols. folio, price 15 guineas. The exact measurements of the Periwigs of the Ancients, taken from the Statues, Bustos, and Basso-Relievos of Athens, Palmyra, Balbec, and Rome, by Modesto, Periwig-maker, from Lagado.

Five rows of perriwigs, faithful portraits we dare be sworn every one, illustrate the Five Orders of Perriwigs. First in order we have the EPISCOPAL, OR PARSONIC WIGS, followed by the OLD PEERIAN OR ALDERMANIC; the LEXONIC; COMPOSITE, *or Half Natural*; and, last of all, the QUEERINTHIAN. The reader will understand from the advertisement given above that the engraving was a notable quiz on Athenian Stuart, as he was called, whose laborious and accurate work on the Antiquities of Athens has been of such service to architects. It is said that the portrait of Stuart, outlined as a wig-block in the original was so unmistakably like the author of the Antiquities that Hogarth struck off the nose on purpose to disguise the joke a little. One of the OLD PEERIAN order of wigs was at once recognized as a hit at the notorious Bubb Doddington, "the last grave fop of the last age:"

> "Who, quite a man of gingerbread,
>
> Savour'd in talk, in dress, and phiz,
>
> More of another world than this."

Bubb Doddington's wig is again figured by Hogarth in one of the prints of "The Election," where it shares in the perils and triumphs of the chairing of the member. Cumberland says that when Doddington was made Lord Melcomb, he actually strutted before the looking-glass, coronet in hand, to study deportment. Warburton's wig was another of the portrait-wigs, of the Parsonic order. From Hogarth's most popular works alone one might select a gallery of wigs—tie-wigs, bag-wigs, pig-tails, and bob-wigs, in every variety—well worthy of earnest criticism. Matthews used to say he wondered what the beggars did with their left off clothes till he went to Ireland, when he discovered some of those old relics curiously clinging to the nakedness of their brethren of the Emerald Isle. What became of the old wigs we had ourselves never sufficiently considered till we scanned one of these said prints, and found, to our delight, what had evidently once been a wig comically seated on the head of a young vagrant beside a gutter.

Voltaire's wig, in the eyes of his contemporaries, was as fatally charged with the electricity of criticism, as Dr. Johnson's proved to be, to the terror of his obsequious followers. This Rhadamanthus of literature, speaking of Geneva, says, "Je secoue ma perruque, la republique est bien poudrée." There was one, André, a perriwig maker, who wrote a play in 1760, and ventured to solicit Voltaire's friendly criticism. His reply is well known; it filled four sides of a sheet of letter-paper with merely a repetition of *"Monsieur André, faites des perruques,"* and ending, *"toujours des perruques et jamais que des perruques."* Descartes had a great passion for perukes; and at the taking of Dresden, Frederick the Great found in the wardrobe of Count Brühl some hundreds of wigs—one authority says fifteen hundred.

Some time before bag-wigs went out of fashion a practical joke was played off in Pall Mall, with the intention of bringing bags into contempt, which had like to have ended somewhat seriously. The particulars are given in the Annual Register of 1761. Some wags dressed up a porter in a bag-wig and lace ruffles, and made him as Frenchified as possible, and drove him into the midst of the fashionable throng in the Mall. His superb dress immediately won the admiration of the votaries of pleasure, who seemed anxious to make his acquaintance; but his absurd conduct soon convinced them of the trick which had been played upon them, and the fellow was thrust out from among them—we sincerely hope with the addition of a good cudgelling.

The time came when perriwig makers had fallen upon evil days. The fashion was evidently on the decline—something must be done for the common good; when, Curtius like, they took a bold leap. Accordingly, on the 11th February, 1765, they presented a petition to his majesty George III., the prayer of which was, that a law should be passed to enforce the wearing of wigs, and that his majesty should help to keep up the fashion. Alas! for the mutability of human affairs, it is questionable if the good king had the power to revive, even for an hour, an expiring fashion: it is certain in this instance, as in others of graver moment, he obstinately adhered to his own choice, and clung to his pig-tail in spite of remonstrance. The London mob, however, proceeded to legislate after their own fashion; and, observing that the wig makers, who wished to make others wear wigs, wore no wigs themselves, they seized hold of the petitioners by force, and cut off all their hair. "Should one wonder," says Horace Walpole, "if carpenters were to remonstrate that since the peace there has been no call for wooden legs." George III. might well be content with his modest pig-tail, which queen Charlotte, like a home-loving wife, as she was, often powdered and bound with ribbon, and curled his majesty's hair in the style he preferred, well knowing in such matters none could please him so well as herself; and thus adorned, we are told, he read the speech from the throne at the meeting of parliament.

At the marriage of the Princess Royal to the Prince of Orange, in the reign of George II., the bridegroom wore a long curled perriwig to hide the terrible hump which disfigured his princely shoulders. As soon as the awkward ceremony was over, the queen gave vent to her feelings in a flood of tears.

The Maccaroni Club, 1772, set the fashion of wearing the hair in a most preposterous style. It was combed upwards into a conical-shaped toupée of monstrous size; and, behind the head, the hair was plaited and tied together into a solid bundle, which of itself must have been an inconvenient load for a gentleman's shoulders. The ladies wore a head-dress of similar altitude, piling Peleon upon Ossa, in the shape of a cushion of horse hair and wool, over which the hair, pomatumed and powdered, was spread out and carried upwards towards the clouds, bedecked with lace and ribbon; the sides of this delectable mountain were ornamented with rows of curls: but words can convey but a very poor idea of this diverting monstrosity. "An you come to sea in a high wind," says Ben to Mrs. Frail, in Congreve's "Love for Love," "you mayn't carry so much sail o' you head—top and top-gallant." And the Macarronies in their day ran the same risk of being capsized by a squall. At the opera these head-dresses so completely intercepted all view of the stage to those in the rear, that, in 1778, a regulation was put in force which excluded them altogether from the amphitheatre.

The amiable Cowper, shocked at the vulgar assurance of the once coy shepherdess, beheld

> "Her head, adorned with lappets pinned aloft,
>
> And ribands streaming gay, superbly raised,
>
> And magnified beyond all human size,
>
> Indebted to some smart wig-weaver's hand
>
> For more than half the tresses it sustains."

Cowper, like Shakspere appears to have entertained a great antipathy to wigs. The author of the Diverting History of John Gilpin assailed them in their dotage: Shakspere would have nipped them in the bud. Cowper, writing to a friend, says, "I give you joy of your own hair. No doubt you are a considerable gainer by being disperriwigged....* * * I have little doubt if an arm or a leg could have been taken off with as little pain as attends the amputation of a curl or a lock of hair, the natural limb would have been thought less becoming than a wooden one."

> "Look on beauty,
>
> And you shall see 'tis purchased by the weight;
>
> Which therein works a miracle in nature,
>
> Making them lightest that wear most of it.
>
> So are the crispéd, snaky, golden locks,
>
> Which make such wanton gambols with the wind,
>
> Upon supposed fairness, often known
>
> To be the dowry of a second head;
>
> The skull that bred them in the sepulchre."

MERCHANT OF VENICE.

The Water-poet was more explicit than elegant when he inveighed against the dames

> "Whose borrowed hair (perhaps not long before)
>
> Some wicked trull in other fashion wore;
>
> Or one that at the gallows made her will,
>
> Late chokéd with the hangman's pickadill;
>
> In which respect a sow, a cat, a mare,
>
> More modest than these foolish females are;
>
> For the brute beasts, (continual night and day,)
>
> Do wear their own still, (and so do not they.)"

Pennant had a strange aversion to wigs, and, when he was half seas over, used to snatch them off the wearers' heads. Once, at Chester, dining with an officer and a personal friend, (who, knowing his particular weakness, purposely sat next him, to prevent mischief,) being somewhat elated with wine, he made a sudden dart at the officer's wig and threw it into the fire. The officer, enraged at the insult, drew his sword, and Pennant took to his heels. The son of Mars was close upon him when Pennant's better knowledge of the bye-ways of Chester stood him in good stead, and he contrived to give the enemy the slip. His friend, who remembered all the particulars of this hair-breadth escape, used to call it Pennant's Tour in Chester.

When Fag, in Sheridan's play of "The Rivals," meets Sir Anthony's coachman at Bath, he tells him he must polish a little, and that "none of the London whips of any degree of ton wear wigs now." But the bucolic mind is eminently conservative, and Thomas makes answer, "Odd's life! when I heard how the lawyers and doctors had took to their own hair, I thought how 'twould go next. Why, bless you, the gentlemen of the professions ben't all of a mind; for in our village now, thoff Jack Gauge, the exciseman, has ta'en to his carrots; there's little Dick, the farrier, swears he'll never forsake his bob, though all the college should appear with their own heads."

It was during the first shock of the French Revolution, when the laws, religion, and social institutions of France were overturned, as by an earthquake, that wigs were discarded with other insignia of the old régime. The heroes of pagan Rome, and the fabled deities of Greece, supplied the French Republicans with models for their newest fashions. The men with rough cropped hair sported a *Brutus*, and the ladies in scanty draperies assumed the coiffure *à la Greque*. While the heroic citizens rejoiced in their newly acquired liberty and freedom from wigs, the chaste matrons went in search of false hair, to imitate the classic beauties of antiquity. In England, however sudden the transformations in high life, the change, agreeably to the genius of the people, was rather the growth of a new system than the uprooting of the old. The old wig decayed slowly beside the growth of a new crop, and lingered long in many a humble circle, became the oracle of the club, and enjoyed the dignity of the arm-chair and the repose of the chimney-corner; and some would be laid up in ordinary with family relics in the old lumber-room, like Uncle Toby's white Ramillies wig in the old campaign trunk, which the corporal put into pipes and furbished up for the grand *coup de main* with widow Wadman, but which resisted all Trim's efforts, and the repeated application of candle-ends, to bring into better curl.

It chanced that Queen Charlotte's auburn locks fell off during her accouchment. At this fatal omen the extravagant head-dresses then in fashion were suddenly sacrificed. Her majesty and the princesses in 1793 were pleased to discard hair-powder, which speedily rid the *beau monde* of that encumbrance. In 1795 the hair-powder tax of one guinea per head, imposed by Pitt's act, came into operation. The tax at one time realized as much as £20,000 per annum. This lessened considerably the number of powdered heads; and hair-powder, once so necessary to the finish of the finest gentleman, fell into disuse, except with a few gentlemen's gentlemen—the Fitz-Jeames in livery.

For state and ceremony except among the lawyers and the bench of bishops, at last nothing worthy the name of a perriwig was left to admire. George the Third's bag-wig was as unpretending as the king himself. His statue beyond Charing Cross will happily remind posterity of that most respectable monarch—and his wig. Dr. Johnson's scratch-wig, of which Boswell has left us a most authentic account, is familiar to most readers. That famous old scratch, too small for his head, always uncombed, and the fore part burnt away by contact with the candle, must be carefully distinguished from the smart wig which Mrs. Thrale's butler kept for him at Streatham and placed on his head as he passed through the hall to dinner.

During the decadence of the wig, the army and navy wore pig-tails, which were nourished with regulation charges of powder and pomatum. How gallantly they defended them, the history of many a well-fought battle can tell—

"Not once or twice in our rough island story,

The path of duty was the way to glory."

In 1804, the soldier's allowance of pig-tail was reduced to seven inches, and in 1808 the order was promulgated to cut them off, but countermanded the very next day. However, revocation was impossible; for the barbers, with their usual alacrity, had performed their stern duties successfully, and not a pig-tail remained to the British army.

Is the reader curious to know something about Sergeants of the coif, and the mysteries of the bar-wig with its rows of curls and twin tails? Let him make his studies from nature, and "the stiff-wigged living figures," as Elia calls them. The sages of the law were among the last to forego the use of wigs in private life; and it is said that Mr. Justice Park acquired the cognomen of *Bushy Park*, from the peculiar fashion of his wig, which he retained long after his brethren of the long robe had forsaken theirs. In the Table-talk of Samuel Rogers there is an anecdote of Lord Ellenborough's wig. The judge was setting out for the circuit, and as Lady Ellenborough wished to accompany him, it was agreed between husband and wife that no band-boxes of any kind would be tolerated; for, when travelling, his lordship had a great aversion to band-boxes. On the journey, however, as the judge was stretching his legs in the carriage, they came in contact with the thing he so cordially detested—a band-box. In an instant his lordship seized hold of it, and threw it out of the window. The carriage stopped, and the footman was about to pick it up, when his lordship called out, "*Drive on!*" Arrived at the county town, when the judge was putting on his robes before going into court, enquiry was made for the wig, which, at the last moment, was nowhere to be found. After much delay, the footman was interrogated by his lordship, "Where *is* my wig?" "Why, my lord," replied the servant, "you threw it out of the window." It seems that her ladyship's maid, envious that a judge's wig should travel so comfortably in its proper case, while some pieces of millinery were in danger of being terribly crushed for want of a larger box, at their last resting place had made an exchange, and put the fright of a wig in a band-box, and the millinery in the wig-box. The most villainous of the wig tribe was certainly the peruke of George the Fourth's reign, which, pretending to imitate the natural hair, was, on that very account, the more detestable, in as much as an ape's features are more ridiculous from bearing some resemblance to a man.

Even the bishops have gradually forsaken the episcopal wig. The Irish bishops do not appear to have worn them. The Honorable Richard Bagot, bishop of Bath and Wells, was the first of our modern bishops who dispensed with the wig. Many years previous to his obtaining the bishopric, the Prince Regent had said to him in a joke, "You are much too handsome a man to wear a wig; remember, whenever I make you a bishop you may dispense with wearing one." However, when the bishop reminded his sovereign that his promise when Regent exempted him from wearing a wig, it was only after much hesitation that the favour was granted. Bishop Bloomfield officiated in an orthodox-peruke at the coronation of William IV.; and more recently in the House of Lords, at times, a solitary wig came forth like a decrepid fly in mid-winter, drowsily contemplating the change and bustle going on around it. For a brief space it walked the earth like a troubled spirit—the reverend fathers have exorcised it, and it is no more seen of men.

When George IV. was king, his were the model whiskers (though false ones) which constituted the standard of perfection. Our continental neighbours, in derision, frequently likened the English whiskers to mutton chops or a string of sausages; but John Bull who is always tolerant of abuse, and goes about matters after his own sturdy fashion, maintained his whiskers with imperturbable gravity. Moore, in one of his humorous poems, thus takes off the vanities of royalty, and it says much for the good sense of the king that he could enjoy the wit of the poet when directed against himself:

"He looks in the glass—but perfection is there,

Wig, whiskers, and chin-tufts all right to a hair;

Not a single *ex*-curl on his forehead he traces—

> For curls are like Ministers, strange as the case is,
>
> The *falser* they are, the more firm in their places."

Some brief notes yet remain to complete the present imperfect sketch, but of too recent date to warrant their insertion here. It is gratifying to know that, under the present glorious and auspicious rule, improvement is taking place in all matters of taste, and that even in the changeful fashions of the day we are much indebted to the refined judgment of our most gracious Queen, VICTORIA, whom may God long preserve to reign over a free and enlightened people.

BARBERS.

CHAPTER V.

Barbers, by common consent, enjoy a most enviable reputation. Both in fact and fiction they are the representatives of shrewdness and good nature; and in some of the choicest literature extant, the sayings and doings of the brethren of the craft are among the best of their kind. It would be a dull world without Figaro.

The barber's shop was for centuries the emporium of gossip, the idler's club; and when the young Roman wished to meet with a rake as pleasure-loving as himself, he sought him at the barber's, possibly to contrive how to steal away some old man's daughter or his money-bags. And thither came the old miser to get his finger-nails clipped, taking care, however, to take the parings away with him. All classes frequented the barber's shop; and we may suppose the lively satirists of old visited the spot, as Molière did the barber of Pezenas, to find material for some of their best sketches of character.

The Roman barbers, it must be confessed, were somewhat garrulous, and their tongues went as nimbly as their shears. Like the moderns, they put a rough cloth round the patient, as we are half inclined to call the customer who submitted to the operation, for we fear their razors were none of the best, for some preferred to have their beards plucked out by means of plasters applied to the face, and then those terrible tweezers completed the work, pulling out the stray hairs the razors or plasters had left behind. Some wealthy men had the duties of the barber performed by their own slaves, but the shops were thronged with customers, and the tonsor was at all times the most obedient and obliging servant of the public. One of the peculiarities of their art was the clicking of the shears, to which Juvenal makes allusion:

"He whose officious scizzors went snip, snip,

As he my troublesome young beard did clip."

Several of these worthies attained to great distinction, and rose from the shop to the senate.

The furniture of a barber's shop, to those who are curious in matters of antiquity, might serve to explain the customs of a very remote period. The basin is mentioned in Ezekiel: it is the *cantherus* of the middle ages, which was of bright copper. From a peculiar soap, *lascivium*, used by the fraternity, we derive the word lather. Washing-balls were used for washing and softening the beard before shaving, and the pomatum in use was known as *capillare*. Various modes of frizzing and plaiting the hair, distinguished by appropriate terms, are alluded to by archæologists; but we turn a deaf ear to such traditions—our lode-star glistens near the barber's pole, Mambrino's helmet, bright with sunny memories of golden romance and the adventures of the knight of La Mancha. There has been some diversity of opinion as to the origin of the well-known barber's pole. The prevalent opinion is probably the true one, that it represents the staff held in the hand by the patient phlebotomized by the barber-surgeon; and that the red ribbon coiled round it represents the tape by which the arm was compressed during the operation. And here, at the threshold, we observe the mystical union between Barbery and Surgery; and hence the dignity and professional honours to which the barbers justly lay claim. Lord Thurlow, in the House of Peers (1797) decorated the barber's pole with somewhat different colours when he stated "that, by a statute then in force, the Barbers and Surgeons were each to use a pole. The barbers were to have theirs blue and white, striped, with no other appendage; but the surgeons', which was the same in other respects, was likewise to have a galley-pot and a red rag, to denote the particular nature of their vocation." Our business is not with the galley-pot, although we love the golden beard of Æsculapius well. We incline to the belief that there were no jealousies between the happy couple at an early period of their union. The fees of both professions were, doubtless, small, and seldom any but minor operations attempted; while, probably, the ignorance of both parties was so nearly balanced as to produce the desired equality so necessary to the concord of the married state. For many long years we know they jogged on together without complaint of any kind; that subsequently, if not very loving, they tolerated each other with due decorum; and that, when at last they got to wrangling and high words, they luckily obtained a divorce.

The barber's basin certainly ranks next in importance to the pole. The basin of the proper form had the usual semi-circle cut out of the brim, that it might fit into the neck; and, in another part, a hollow place, like a little dish, to hold the soap: its office was two-fold, and was in requisition both for bleeding and shaving. To the disturbed vision of Don Quixote the brass basin glittered like burnished gold. His adventure with the village barber, mounted on his dappled grey ass, the renowned helmet, and the part it played in the astounding feats of that flower of chivalry, are known the world over, and are among the most pleasant associations connected with the barber's trade. At a public festival in Holland, in honour of the Earl of Leicester, Holinshed says a barber set up some three score of bright copper basins on a wall, with a wax candle burning in each, and a painting of a rose and crown, and an inscription in Latin, "this made a faire shew, and was a pretie deuise." If the fellow were an honest patriot, he deserved a pyramid of brass basins for a monument.

Punning inscriptions and quaint devices outside of the shop were frequently adopted as alluring bait for the lovers of odd whims and fancies, who thought none the worse of the man for having some spice of humour in his composition. Over a barber's shop Hogarth has set up this inscription, "Shaving, bleeding, and teeth drawn with a touch, ECCE SIGNUM." Bat Pigeon, of whom honourable mention is made by both Steele and Addison, had a curious device of a bat and a pigeon, which, in its day, attracted much attention. The wig-maker's sign of Absalom hanging from the oak by his hair, and the darts of Joab fixed in his side, is probably of French origin. The story is told of a barber at Troyes, and the inscription runs thus:

> "Passans, contemplez la douleur
>
> D'Absalon pendu par la nuque:
>
> Il eût évité ce malheur
>
> S'il avait porté la *perruque*."

The English version is more concise:

> "O Absalom, unhappy sprig,
>
> Thou shouldst have worn a perriwig."

The barber's chair may be regarded as the centre of the system. The proverb "As common as a barber's chair" is well known, and Shakspere's clown adds "it fits all buttocks"—the word is not ours—the seat of honour, if you please, reader, furnished with twin cushions to protect the sacred Luz, out of which the Rabbins say the renewed mammal is to sprout forth at the resurrection, as you are probably aware. In old prints, the chattels of a barber's shop are usually few and mean enough; but the chair—the descendant of the *sella tonsoria*—bears some rude flourishes of art, is broad and massive and well-cushioned, as became the throne of so many grave potentates. One is as much astonished at the size of the combs, scissors, and razors of the ancient barbers as at the giant arms and armour worn by the knights of old. What ponderous blades these artists wielded it is fearful to contemplate. There is an old joke that some barber advertised shaving by the acre, and cutting blocks with a razor one would think not impossible with such weapons. Actius' razor, which was of the keenest, must have been after this fashion. As razors are of very old date, it may interest some one to know that, long before Sheffield or Sheffield blades were thought of, Palermo did business in their commodity. The presiding deity was not unfrequently the greatest curiosity about the place. A certain knack of snapping the fingers was a common practice among them; tradition says, it recalled to mind the clicking of the shears used by their great ancestors. Morose, in Ben Jonson's "Silent Woman," so detested this sound, as indeed he did noises of all kind, that meeting with a barber who was without this trick of his profession, he thought it so eminent a virtue, that he made him chief of his counsel, which reminds one of Adrian's rebuke to his gossip of a barber, who, in reply to the man's query how he should like to be shaved, said—silently! But barber's were better employed than in curing the ill-humours of the Morose family. In Stubbes' Anatomie of Abuses (1583) is a dialogue about old barbers, which we will in part transcribe:

"There are no finer fellowes under the sunne, nor experter in their noble science of barbing than they be; and therefore, in the fulness of their overflowing knowledge, (oh! ingenious heads, and worthy to be dignified with the diademe of folly and vain curiositie!) they have invented such strange fashions and monstrous manners of cutting, trimmings, shavings, and washings, that you would wonder to see.... Besides that, when they come to the cutting of the haire, what snipping and snapping of the cycers is there, what tricking and trimming, what rubbing, what scratching, what combing and clawing, what trickling and toying, and all to tawe out money, you may be sure. And when they come to washing, oh! how gingerly they behave themselves therein; for then shall your mouth be bossed with the lather or fome that riseth of the balles (for they have their sweete balles wherewithall they use to washe); your eyes closed must be anointed therewith also. Then snap go the fingers; ful bravely, God wot. Thus, this tragedy ended, comes me warme clothes to wipe and dry him withall; next the eares must be picked and closed togither againe artificially forsooth; the hair of nostrils cut away, and every thing done in order comely to behold. The last action in this tragedie is the paiment of monie. And least these cunning barbers might seem unconscionable in asking much for their paines, they are of such a shamefast modestie, as they will ask nothing at all, but, standing to the curtesie and liberalitie of the giver, they will receive all that comes, how much soever it be, not giving anie again, I warrant you; for take a barber with that fault, and strike off his head. No, no, such fellows are *Raræ in terris, nigrisque simillimi cygnis*,—"Rare birds upon the earth, and as geason as black swans." You shall have also your Orient perfumes for your nose, your fragrant waters for your face, wherewith you shall bee all to besprinkled: your musicke againe, and pleasant harmonie shall sound in your eares, and all to tickle the same with vaine delight. And in the end your cloke shall be brushed, and, God be with you, gentleman!...* * * * * * But yet I must needs say (these nisities set apart) barbers are verie necesarie, for otherwise men should grow verie ougglisom and deformed, and their haire would in processe of time overgrowe their face, rather like monsters, than comlie sober Christians."

Stubbes, himself, was an inveterate trifler—one of an army of pigmies warring against cranes; but we acquit him of all malice; he belonged to that numerous class who originate nothing, but find fault with everything—

"The long-neck'd geese of the world for ever hissing dispraise

Because their natures are little,"

as Tennyson calls them. An apt turn for flattery was very requisite in an accomplished barber—one of the most difficult things, by the way, for humanity to attain to; for if satire should wound, like a keen razor, "with a touch that's scarcely felt or seen," flattery, like rouge, should be applied with a very delicate hand, indeed. Suckling's verses allude to this hazardous feat:

"When I'm at work, I'm bound to find discourse

To no great purpose, of great Sweden's force,

Of Witel, and the Burse, and what 'twill cost

To get that back which was this summer lost.

So fall to praising of his lordship's hair,

Ne'er so deformed, I swear 'tis *sans* compare:

I tell him that the King's does sit no fuller,

And yet his is not half so good a colour:

Then reach a pleasing glass, that's made to lye

Like to its master most notoriously:

And if he must his mistress see that day,

I with a powder send him strait away."

But other duties such as bleeding, cupping, and drawing teeth had to be attended to in turn. Those who have seen the

"Black rotten teeth in order strung,

Rang'd cups, that in the window stood,

Lin'd with red rags to look like blood,"

will acknowledge that this was once a very important branch of industry. We have ourselves seen the tooth of some unknown animal in a collection of the kind, which, for size, would have astonished Professor Owen; the sight of it, we were told, had frightened away many a toothache. The reader has probably met with the anecdote of Queen Elizabeth, who hesitated about having a tooth drawn; when Bishop Aylmer sat down in the chair, and said to the operator, "Come, though I am an old man, and have but few teeth to spare, draw me this!" which was done; and the queen, seeing him make so slight a matter of it, sat down and had hers drawn, also.

When it was part of the popular belief that the human subject required to be bled at regular intervals to ensure good health and make the ladies fair, and when every barber-surgeon was ready "to breathe a vein," we may be sure the lancet was in constant request. Cupping was recommended to remove a catarrh or cold in the head; and one who made trial of its virtues says, he was startled by being asked by the operator if he wished to be *sacrificed*; but declined being scarified on that occasion. We take it for granted there must have been uncommon stamina in the British constitution, or it would long since have broken down hopelessly under the rough handling it has undergone.

Benjamin Suddlechop, in Scott's "Fortunes of Nigel," has become the model barber of our popular literature; the sketch is confessedly a slight one, and, indeed, after Cervantes, Fielding, Smollett, and Le Sage—not to mention others—have given their delineations of the character, the barbers stand in need of no further help to fame. Even Suddlechop had some music in his soul; his shop in Fleet-street resounded with the tinklings of the guitar, where the lover, if so inclined, might warble "a woeful ballad to his mistress' eyebrows," or flay some spell-bound Marsyas with sounds by no means

> "As sweet and musical
>
> As bright Apollo's lute, strung with his hair."

But what shall we say to Suddlechop's little back shop, from which he supplied his customers with strong waters. We consider this a sad blot upon his fame. Many of the barbers sold cordials and compounded English *aqua-vitæ*, and to them we are indebted for some of the earliest recipes for British brandy—an abominable mixture, which, like the filthy poison known as gin, has destroyed more victims than ever groaned under the lancet of the barber-surgeon. Could these worthies have foreseen what scandalous things would come of this gin drinking, how

> "The vitriol madness flashes up in the ruffian's head,
>
> Till the filthy by-lane rings to the yell of the trampled wife,"

what disease, and want, and wretchedness, and crime, are engendered of this poison to men's souls—all to build up the fortunes of a few wealthy capitalists—we are sure even the strong nerves of the dashing barber would have failed him, and he would have turned with loathing from the hateful traffic. Rabelais makes Pope Calixtus a woman's barber in the other world, which might be a very salutary discipline for a proud pontiff; and we put it to the prince of jovial drinkers himself to suggest any more fitting purgatorial chastisement for the gin-fire aristocracy, than that of compelling them to drink their own vile compounds: Prometheus, bound to the rock, with the vulture preying on his liver, would be but a faint type of their misery.

Before we dismiss Suddlechop, we have to remark that though dame Ursula, his wife, carried on the sale of cosmetics and perfumes, and dealt in other mysteries in her own room at hand, the business of a perfumer, as the term is now understood, had nothing to do with the ancient craft of barbery; such matters concerned St. Veronica and the milliners—the barbers and their patron saint, St. Louis, were engaged on higher mysteries. To preserve order, or, more probably, to promote merriment, a list of forfeits was hung up in the shop; those who chose to pay them did, and those who did not might laugh at them—

> "like the forfeits in a barbers shop,
>
> As much in mock as mark."

Some old-fashioned "rules for seemly behaviour" have been handed to certain learned antiquaries as genuine regulations of the craft; but old birds are not to be caught with chaff, and the archæologist knows better. The forfeits are said to have been incurred by meddling with the razors, talking about cutting throats, swearing, pricking another with the spurs, taking another's turn, interrupting the barber, and such like venial offences. It was formerly the custom to apply the soap with the hand when lathering the beard; the practice of using a brush was a French innovation, not known in England till the year 1756. Nor must we omit to mention that contrivance of the dark ages, the barber's candlestick, which consisted of an upright wooden stem, pointed at the lower end, which was fixed in the apron string, and a projecting branch moveable round the stem to hold the candle.

Down even to the time of Queen Anne the barber's shop was frequented by the better sort of people, and the hand that trimmed the tradesman curled the courtier. In Green's "Quip for an Upstart Courtier," (1592), we read, "With quaint terms you greet Master Velvet-breeches withal, and at every word a snap with your scissors, and a cringe with your knee; whereas, when you come to poor Cloth-breeches, you either cut his beard at your own pleasure, or else in disdain ask him if he will be trimmed with Christ's cut, round like the half of a Holland cheese?"

Some of the old histories afford curious glimpses of the varied fortunes of the trade. In the time of Henry VI., the king's palace was surrounded by little barbers' shops, under the direction of the barber of the household. There being then no carriages, and the streets being dirty, it is probable that those who went to court were first shaved and dressed in these shops. A considerable fee was given to this barber for shaving every Knight of the Bath, on his creation; forty shillings from every baron; one hundred shillings from every earl; and ten pounds from every duke. The barbers of London were first incorporated by King Edward IV., in 1461, and at that time were the only persons who practised surgery. In France the Company of Barbers dates from 1096. An association called the Company of Surgeons was then formed prior to the act of Henry VIII., regulating the trade of barbers and surgeons. This act incorporated the company of surgeons with the barbers, under the name of the Barbers and Surgeons of London, and defined the duties of both professions: the barbers were not to practice surgery further than drawing of teeth, and the surgeons were strictly prohibited from exercising the craft of shaving. It is needless to add, that to a much later period, any act of parliament to the contrary notwithstanding, the barber did as much of the surgeon's work as he could get. In certain articles devised by Henry VIII. for the establishment of good order in his household and chambers, there is an order by which the king's barber is "expressly enjoined to be cleanly, and by no means to frequent the company of idle persons and misguided women, for fear of danger to the king's most royal person."

Montaigne complains (1581) that throughout Italy he had not been able to get hold of a single barber that could either shave him, or cut, or arrange his hair properly. The barber of King Charles II. seems to have acquired somewhat of the levity of his master, (evil communications corrupt good manners); for one day, while shaving him, with his usual familiarity he hazarded the remark, that none of his majesty's officers had a greater trust than himself. "How so, friend?" quoth the king. "Why," said the barber, "I could cut your majesty's throat whenever I liked." Charles started up at the idea, and, using his favourite oath, exclaimed, "Odds fish, the very thought is treason!" Nor could King Charles have forgotten the occasion when William Penderel first performed the office of barber, and shaved and trimmed him in a very sorry fashion, that he might elude his enemies. Royalty must at all times have been a very awkward customer for the barber to meddle with. Midas' barber who appears to have had the *cacoethes loquendi* which is said to be endemic with the craft, suffered dreadfully in consequence. Fortunately for a few crowned heads, the tonsor, taught discretion by the story of Midas, has become the most prudent of men, and not a whisper is uttered on earth of any peculiar developement about the ears which the Phrygian cap effectually conceals from the vulgar.

Female barbers were not unknown to our forefathers, and, till within a few years, were to be met with in the provinces: possibly some "weird sisters" still survive in odd localities. We remember a sturdy little Welsh woman who wielded the razor very successfully in her native town, and was patronized extensively by the sailors and quarrymen. The five barberesses of Drury Lane, who dreadfully maltreated a woman in the reign of Charles II., are remembered for their infamy. Local histories tell of a noted barberess in Seven Dials, and of a black woman who did duty at Butcher Row, near the Temple. The delicate manipulation of female artists is proverbial; but one shudders at the thought of encountering the armed hand of the female barber; for who has forgotten the trick which the barber-damsel put upon Don Quixote, when she raised a lather a span high, covering up his face and beard with a white foam, and then left him for awhile with his neck outstretched, and his eyes half shut, "the strangest and most ridiculous figure imaginable;" and how poor Sancho was threatened with still worse consequences, and protested loudly against the beard-scouring by the scullions, adding, with his usual shrewdness, that there was no such difference between him and his master, that one should be washed with angel water and the other with devil's-ley. Southey informs us that female shavers were not uncommon in Spain in his day. The more feminine occupation of hair-dressing was long carried on by the other sex, in a becoming and artistic manner: witness the announcement of one of them, copied by Strutt from the original in the British Museum:—

A   R

Next Door to the Golden Bell, St. Bride's Lane, Fleet Street,

LYVETH LYDIA BEERCRAFT,

Who cutteth and curleth ladies, gentlemen, and children's hair.—She sells a fine pomatum, which is mix'd with ingredients of her own makeing, that if the hair be never so thin, it makes it grow thick; and if short, it makes it grow long. If any gentleman's or children's hair be never so lank, she makes it curle in a little time, and to look like a perriwig.

It will be observed in Queen Anne's reign no other style but that of the perriwig was thought worthy of imitation. In former times, the university barber was a person of some consequence. The vice-chancellor and proctors invited the fraternity to an annual supper, and no barber or hair-dresser could exercise his vocation in the university unless he matriculated,—took the usual oath, and had his name entered on the books of the university. It was usual for the college barber to wait upon the "freshmen," and dress and powder them in the prevailing fashion—a custom which Southey was among the first to resist—an innovation he would scarcely have ventured on in after life.

The home of the first Company of Barber-Surgeons in London was probably where the hall of their successors, the barbers, is at this day, in Monkwell Street. The present building was erected by subscription some years after the Fire of London, which all but consumed its predecessor: a portion of the hall, of a semicircular shape, is actually within one of the bastions, still entirely perfect, of the old Roman wall—the ancient boundary of the metropolis. The court-room, designed by Inigo Jones, though small, is of fine proportions, and contains what must now be considered the chief riches of the company—a noble painting by Holbein, "Henry VIII. granting the charter to the Barber-Surgeons"—one of the finest pictures by Holbein in this country. There is also a portrait of Inigo Jones, by Vandyke; a picture by Sir Peter Lely, and other valuable paintings. The Company possesses a silver-gilt cup, presented by Henry VIII.; another the gift of Charles II.; and a large bowl given by Queen Anne. Such are some of the relics the barbers may still feel proud of, which we trust are not fated to decay; but, as this is eminently an age of revival and restoration, it is to be hoped the old hall may yet see better days; that, whatever was garnered up of old by the wisdom and prudence of our forefathers, may be wisely and liberally enjoyed by this generation, and the good work carried on and extended for a later age. The arms of the barbers are:—

Quarterly first and fourth, *sa*, a chevron between three fleams *ar*, second and third, per pale *ar*, and vert, a spatula in pale *ar*, surmounted of a rose, *gu*, charged with another of the first; the first rose regally crowned *proper*. Between the four quarters a cross of St. George, *gu*, charged with a lion passant gardant, *or*. *Crest*—An opinicus, with wings indorsed, *or*. *Supporters*—Two lynxes *proper*, spotted of various colours, both ducally collared and chained, *or*. *Motto*—"De præscientia Dei."

If we were privileged to direct our thoughts to other lands, and to record the pleasant life of that admirable humourist, the barber of Southern Europe, we might hope to add a little sunshine to these pages. Who enjoys life better than Figaro—who is as well entertained—who is half as entertaining?

Ah che bel vivere!

Che bel piacere per un barbiere di qualita,

Ah bravo Figaro, bravo bravissimo fortunatissimo.

What a lively, sensuous, *al fresco* life he has of it at Naples; content, without the semblance of property of any kind; in action, free as the breeze; and in spirit, buoyant as a wave.

Ah che bel vivere!

But the shrine of Figaro must be sought in Seville. In the charming fictions of Cervantes and Le Sage, we seem to live on most familiar terms with the Spanish barber, as much so, as with Smollett's Hugh Strap, or Partridge in Fielding's "Tom Jones." So truthfully is the invisible world peopled for us by the power of genius. Romance seems in some way associated with the character of a barber—

"In Venice, Tasso's echoes are no more,

And songless rows the silent gondolier;"

but the barber still contrives an occasional serenade, accompanying his amorous tinklings with vocal strains which would rouse the Seven Sleepers. What a contrast to his European brethren is the grave barber of the East, who is usually physician, astrologer, and barber, and better known to most of us by the amusing story in the Arabian Nights than from any other source. Much might be said of Yankee wit and humour in the person of the American barber; something too, of the crude state of the art in Africa, where, to complete her modest coiffure, the sable beauty is seated in the sun with a lump of fat on her head, which trickles down in resplendent unctuous streams with a profusion enough to make a railway engine jealous. Nor can we stop to notice the Chinese "one piccie Barber-man," whose speculations on heads and tails must be highly amusing; for the Fates are inexorable, and our canvass too small to complete the picture.

We must not, however, omit all mention of the trade in human hair, on which the wig-maker is dependent for his supplies. Ovid alludes to this traffic— light and auburn hair was most sought for by the Roman ladies which was brought from Germany and the North of Europe—

"Hair is good merchandise, and grown a trade,

Markets and public traffic thereof made;

Nor do they blush to cheapen it among

The thickest number, and the rudest throng."

In the reign of Elizabeth, the wearing of false hair was something of a novelty; Italian ladies of no reputation are said to have first revived the fashion. Stubbes took up the cudgels in earnest; he says:—

"They are not simply content with their own hair, but buy other hair, either of horses, mares, or any other strange beasts, dyeing of what colour they list themselves. And if there be any poor woman (as now and then we see—God doth bless them with beauty as well as the rich) that have fair hair, these nice dames will not rest till they have bought it. Or if any children have fair hair, then will entice them into a secret place, and for a penny or two they will cut off their hair; as I heard that one did in the city of Londinium of late who, meeting a little child with very fair hair, inveigled her into a house, promised her a penny and so cut off her hair."

In more modern times the demand has created a distinct branch of trade, and various agencies are at work to procure the needful supply. Black hair comes principally from Brittany and the South of France, where it is collected by dealers who visit the principal fairs, and barter ribbons, kerchiefs, and such matters, for the tresses of the Breton lasses. From a superstitious feeling, most of them are averse to take money for their hair, and consider it unlucky to do so. As it is an invariable custom for the females to wear a close cap from childhood, the loss of their magnificent *chignons* is thereby concealed. Germany supplies the market, as of old, with light and flaxen hair, and this branch of trade is chiefly carried on by a Dutch company. The London hair-dressers alone, purchase some five tons annually. The annual consumption in Great Britain of foreign human hair is assumed to be about six tons. Hair which curls naturally, and is of good colour and very fine, commands the highest price; and certain shades, which are comparatively rare, are much sought for. Such choice lots are packed up in skins, to exclude the air, and exported to the best markets. Fashion, however, has much to do in regulating the price. Bryant, the American poet, whose Pegasus seems to have taken fright at the gaudeous dresses of the beauties in the Broadway, thus discourses of hair with a poet's license:

> "And thick about those lovely temples lie
>
> Locks that the lucky Vignardonne has curled.
>
> Thrice happy man! whose trade it is to buy,
>
> And bake, and braid those love-knots of the world;
>
> Who curls of every glossy colour keepest,
>
> And sellest, it is said, the blackest cheapest.
>
> And well thou mayst—for Italy's brown maids

Send the dark locks with which their brows are dressed,

And Gascon lasses, from their jetty braids,

Crop half, to buy a riband for the rest;

And the fresh Norman girls their tresses spare,

And the Dutch damsel keeps her flaxen hair.

Then, henceforth, let no maid nor matron grieve,

To see her locks of an unlovely hue,

Grizzled or thin, for liberal art shall give

Such piles of curls as nature never knew.

Eve, with her veil of tresses, at the sight

Had blushed, outdone, and owned herself a fright."

When long-curled perriwigs were in fashion, some fine heads of hair fetched extraordinary prices; and as it was impossible to find human hair in sufficient quantity for the purposes of trade, recourse was had to horse-hair. One of the companies projected just before the bursting of the South Sea bubble, was a company for dealing in human hair which promised unheard of profits. In "A Description of Trades," published 1747, we are told, "that the business of hair-curlers and sellers is properly a part of perriwig making, but of late years they have prevailed so much as to become quite a separate trade, and really not an inconsiderable one neither, some of them being even styled *merchants*, who have the makers-up of hair in all shapes for their customers. There are also abundance of hawkers and pedlars who go up and down the country to buy up this commodity, who generally dispose of it to these hair-sellers." The material for a perriwig being somewhat costly, and trickery not uncommon, the character of the barber was the best guarantee for the quality of the wig. The reader has probably heard how Tom Brown, meeting a parson at Nando's Coffee-house, recommended him to the honestest perriwig-maker in Christendom—the barber at Chelmsford, with his nineteen daughters, all bred up to his own trade, and being kept unmarried, their hair grew so prodigiously fast that it gave them full employment throughout the year; the barber cropped them every four years, and never lacked a plentiful harvest—so that Chelmsford was as famous for its wigs, as Romford for calves. The girls were all virtuous, which made the hair the stronger, and there was not finer hair to be had in the kingdom. On this, the parson who was in want of a new wig, and had been cheated in his last purchase, set out for Chelmsford, and returned thoroughly satisfied—that he had been sent on a fool's errand.

The value of long fair hair, when wigs were in fashion, is amusingly shown in Walpole's anecdote of the Countess of Suffolk, married to Mr. Howard. "Such was their poverty, that having invited some friends to dinner, and being disappointed of a small remittance, she was forced to sell her hair to furnish the entertainment, and for which she obtained twenty pounds." Middle Row, Holborn, was chiefly inhabited by perriwig-makers, and the French barbers congregated in Soho.

One of the mysteries of the craft was the art of dyeing hair, and every barber was supposed to be fully initiated in this occult science. Greeks and Romans performed similar feats in their day, but blonde hair being most esteemed, the compositions they used were of a very different nature to those employed by the moderns; strictly speaking they could hardly be called dyes, they partook more of the nature of caustic pomades and pigments: such were the *pilæ Mattiacæ*, the *caustica spuma*, *spuma Battava*, &c., of their authors, imported for the most part from Germany. Making old folks young again, at least in appearance, was not beyond the power of Roman art, for the locks of age, white as the plumage of the swan, could be suddenly changed to that of a crow. Sir Thomas Brown suggests that Medea might have possessed some famous dye:—"That Medea, the famous sorceress, could renew youth, and make old men young again, was nothing else but that, from the knowledge of simples, she had a receipt to make white hair black, and reduce old heads into the tincture of youth again." Mohammed forbade the dyeing of the hair; and a story is told of Herod, that in order to conceal his advanced age, he used secretly to dye his grey locks with a dark pigment In the greater number of Anglo-Saxon M.S.S. the hair and beard are painted blue, and sometimes green and orange. Strutt concluded from this, that the Saxons dyed or tinged their hair in some way; but the point is doubtful. In the fourteenth century, yellow was the favourite colour, and saffron was used as a dye. Again, in Elizabeth's reign, fair hair became fashionable, and the ladies used various compositions to obtain the desired shade. Stubbes is indignant at the practice, and exclaims with his usual warmth:—"If any have hair of their own natural growing which is not fair enough, then will they dye it in divers colours, almost changing the substance into accidents by their devilish, and worse than these, cursed devices." Foreign charlatans, quack doctors, and astrologers, were formidable rivals of the barber, and succeeded in disposing of their dyes and cosmetics in the most unblushing manner; some affected to be so occupied in the sublime study of contriving cures for all the ills which flesh is heir to, as to have no leisure for cosmetic practice, and coolly announced that their wives attended to such matters. A high German doctor and astrologer informed the public that he was blessed with a wife "who could make red hair as white as a lily, shape the eyebrows to a miracle, make low foreheads as high as you please, and had a rich water which would make the hair curl." The practice of shaping the eyebrows, though now in disuse, was at one time considered a very delicate and important operation. Every one has remarked the extreme fineness of the eyebrows in the pictures of the great Italian masters. The St. Catherine of Rafaelle, and the Saints of Francia, in the National Gallery, are instances of this; such was the fashion of the Italian ladies of the fifteenth century, and was esteemed a great beauty. The eyebrows were carefully reduced in substance to a mere line, till scarcely visible. A lady, whose lover had an unconquerable aversion to red hair, once made application to a noted quack, who, politely answered:—"This is no business of mine, but my wife's, who'll soon redress your grievances, and furnish you with a leaden comb and my *Anti-Erythræan Unguent*, which after two or three applications will make you as fair or as brown as you desire." We hope, for the ladies sake, it turned out to be the true *Elisir d'amore*. A Mr. Michon, a goldsmith, in 1710, advertised a clear fluid, which would change red or grey hair to brown or black, under the name of "The Tricosian Fluid." The remarkable success which attended the use of the *Cyananthropopoion*, patronized by Titmouse Tittlebat, is known to all readers of "Ten Thousand a Year." It would, however, say but little for the progress of chemistry in our day, if we were unprovided with some efficient means of dyeing the hair; in competent hands, no doubt, the thing is easy enough. The old-fashioned dyes are now perfectly useless, and may safely be consigned to the same limbo with Peter Pindar's razors:

"Sir," quoth the razor man, "I'm not a knave;

  As for the razors you have bought,—

  Upon my soul, I never thought

That they *would* shave."

"Not shave" cries Hodge, with wondering, staring eyes,

  And voice not much unlike an Indian yell—

"What were they made for, then, you knave?" he cries.

  "Made," quoth the fellow, with a smile, "*to sell.*"

The names of no inconsiderable number of barbers are inscribed on the roll of Fame. In the very foremost rank we may place that of the poor barber, Arkwright, who lived to accomplish such great things for the trade of this country. His was an instance of that material success which the dullest can comprehend, and the vulgarest worshipper of Mammon will stand agape at. To be knighted by the Sovereign, and to realize half a million of money, would be fame enough for most ambitious minds—but this is but dust in the balance, compared with the value of the vast enterprise to which the barber's talents gave the first impulse. Wealth, beyond the dreams of avarice, has accrued from that giant industry; and yet rival manufacturers would have crushed him if they could, so blind is grasping selfishness to its own true interests. Till the age of twenty-eight, Arkwright worked at the barber's trade, then turned dealer in hair, which he travelled about to collect and dispose of to the trade. A hair-dye he happened to get hold of was a source of considerable profit to him. But his good genius was at hand to rescue him from obscurity, and although his subsequent career appeals but little to the imagination, his fame will long endure to attest the energy and the capability of the British workman. Belzoni was another earnest spirit working out its freedom in a different way. His adventurous career is well known; had it not been for the promptings of an active mind, he might have lived and died shaving beards at Padua. Burchiello, the Florentine, gave up the razor, and courted the Muse, as he says in one of his sonnets;

"La Poesia combatti col rasio."

Jasmin, the French poet of Agen, rose from extreme poverty to comfort and independence as a barber, and acquired a well-earned reputation by his pleasant verses "Les Papillotes," and the Poem "L'Aveugle de Castel Cuillé." Allan Ramsey must be numbered with the barber poets; and literature is indebted to Winstanley, a barber of the time of Charles II., for his "Lives of the English Poets." These, however, have earned other titles than those conferred by their original calling; there are others, whose sole claim to notice is their professional reputation. Among the most noted barbers of their day we may mention "the gentleman barber" to the Earl of Pembroke, who built a large house with tennis-courts and bowling-green, nick-named Shaver's Hall, the resort of the gayest of the nobility, where many a fortune was lost and won; and Farr who opened the well-known coffee-house, "The Rainbow," in Fleet Street, hard by Temple Bar. Lillie who had a shop at the corner of Beaufort Buildings, in the Strand, whose fame is preserved in the pages of the Tatler and Spectator. Honest Bat Pigeon, of whom Steele and Addison make honourable mention. Gregory, the famous peruke-maker, from whom the wig called a "Gregorian" took its name, and who lies buried in the church of St. Clement Danes, with an epitaph in rhyme, writ, says Aubrey, by a Baron of the Exchequer. Shammeree, the fashionable wig-maker of the reign of William III.; and Stewart, the author of the "The Noble Art of Hair-dressing." Amid minor celebrities, Don Saltero occupies a conspicuous place—he opened his museum-coffee-house, in Cheyne Walk, Chelsea, in 1695. Sir Hans Sloane supplied him with many curiosities for his museum. His own name was James Salters. He claimed to have some skill on the fiddle, could draw a tooth, made most excellent punch, and was esteemed a virtuoso and a wit. He includes himself among the oddities at the Chelsea Knackatory, with much complacency, in the following verses:

Through various employs I've past—

    A scraper, virtuos' projector,

Tooth-drawer, trimmer, and at last

    I'm now a gim-crack-whim collector;

Monsters of all sorts here are seen,

    Strange things in nature as they grew so:

Some relics of the Sheba Queen,

    And fragments of the fam'd Bob Crusoe;

Knick-knacks, too, dangle round the wall,

    Some in glass cases, some on shelf;

But, what's the rarest sight of all,

    Your humble servant shows himself—

On this my chiefest hope depends.

    Now, if you will my cause espouse,

In Journals pray direct your friends

    To my Museum-Coffee-house;

And in requital for the timely favour,

    I'll gratis bleed, draw teeth, and be your shaver.

Steele, alluding to Don Saltero, asks, "why must a barber be for ever a politician, a musician, an anatomist, a poet, and a physician?" He was evidently puzzled to account for the varied talents of the brotherhood.

The sons of barbers have, likewise, achieved great distinction: we may instance Jeremy Taylor, secretary Craggs, the friend of Addison; Tonson, the publisher; Turner, the painter; and Lord Tenterden. We are told by one whose testimony we cannot doubt, that when Lord Tenterden visited Canterbury in company with his son, he took him to the very spot where his own father had carried on his humble trade, and said, "Charles, you see this little shop; I have brought you here on purpose to show it you. In that shop your grandfather used to shave for a penny! That is the proudest reflection of my life! While you live never forget that, my dear Charles." Lord St.

Leonards, we believe, rose from a sphere equally humble, and his father followed the same trade. Lord Campbell has rescued the name of "Dick Danby" from oblivion by a kindly notice in one of his volumes, "One of the most intimate friends I have ever had:" says his lordship, "was Dick Danby, who kept a hair-dresser's shop under the Cloisters in the Inner Temple. He could tell who were getting on and who were without a brief, who succeeded by their talents and who hugged the attorneys, who were desirous of becoming puisne judges, and who meant to try their fortune in parliament, which of the chiefs was in a failing state of health, and who was next to be promoted to the collar of S.S. Poor fellow! he died suddenly, and his death threw a universal gloom over Westminster Hall, unrelieved by the thought that the survivors who mourned him might pick up some of his business— a consolation which wonderfully softens the grief felt for the loss of a favourite Nisi Prius leader." We may conclude by quoting the words of the same learned author:—"Although there be something exciting to ridicule in the manipulations of barbers, according both to works of fiction and the experience of life, there is no trade which furnishes such striking examples of ready wit, of entertaining information, and of agreeable manners."

STRUCTURE, GROWTH,
AND
COLOUR OF THE HAIR.

CHAPTER VI.

In olden time, the hair was said to be produced by "a vapour or excrement of the brain." In the more exact language of science it is described as a horny appendage of the skin. The skin is shown to be composed of two layers—the outer termed the cuticle, the inner the cutis. The cuticle is an insensible transparent membrane covering the whole surface of the body; the portion exposed to the air consists of flattened cells or scales which are continually being renewed; while on the inner surface, in contact with the cutis, is a soft mucous substance, in which are situate the pigment cells giving the characteristic colour peculiar to race and climate. The cutis is composed of the layer of minute papillæ, the principal seat of the sense of touch, covering an intricate arrangement of fibrous tissue, which receives the delicate ramifications of the nerves and arteries. The sheath from which the hair protrudes above the skin is formed by a tubular depression of the cuticle which reaches below the cutis to the subjacent fat and cellular tissue; the lower end of the sheath is shaped like a pouch, and contains the pulp from which the bulb and shaft of the hair are formed in successive portions—the most recent pushing forward that previously formed. The bulbs are larger in young than in old hairs, and are implanted obliquely in respect to the cuticle. The shaft of the hair being formed by an aggregation of parts, has been likened to a pile of thimbles one resting within the other; this overlapping of the outer coating of scales gives rise to that roughness which we feel on passing the fingers along a hair from the point to the bulb, though apparently perfectly smooth when held in the opposite direction. The colouring matter of the hair is seen in the pulp, and is distributed between the cells composing the shaft. In form the hair may be described as a flattened cylinder, not, however, hollow or filled with a kind of pith as is usually supposed; but solid throughout and formed of a homogeneous mass of a cellular texture. From the extreme minuteness of its structure, and the mystery which shrouds all vital processes, it is still a question as to whether the shaft of the hair is permeable by fluids derived from the blood. The old notion of a circulation within the hair like the sap in vegetables is disregarded; but it is contended that absorption does take place, and that fluids are transmitted to the extreme point of the hair. In proof of this we are referred to the sudden change of colour which the hair undergoes in extraordinary cases of mental emotion, as instanced in the sufferings of Marie Antoinette, whose hair was found to have turned grey with grief. It is assumed that the altered condition of the blood acting chemically upon the fluids of the hair destroys the colour. If this be granted, we must look for minor changes in the colour of the hair with every ordinary change in the normal condition of the blood. And we are told this does actually take place; that in health the hair is glossy, brilliant, and rich in hue; in ill health dry, faded, blank, and withered. But if this be so, and the connection between the blood and fluids of the hair be thus intimate, how comes it that partial changes of colour—this paleness of hue, and loss of brilliancy; and on the other hand, increased depth of colour consequent on renewed health—are not common phenomena and familiar to every one? Doubtless, we have still much to learn of the secrets of Nature, and there is yet something wanting to complete the revelations of the microscope, and the teachings of physiologists respecting the hair.

The palms of the hands and the soles of the feet are the only portions of the skin unfurnished with hairs. Their length and thickness varies considerably, from the softest down which is scarcely visible, to the long hair of the scalp and beard. The estimated thickness of a hair of the head is one-tenth of a line. Observations seem to show that flaxen is the finest, and black the coarsest hair. In females the hair of the head ordinarily measures from twenty to thirty inches, but in some instances it attains a much greater length; and mention is made of ladies whose hair has been two yards long and reached to the ground when they stood erect. The beard has been known to grow to the enormous length of nine feet: the portrait of a carpenter with a beard of this length, is preserved at Eidam; when at work he was obliged to pack it up in a bag. We are told the Burgomeister Hans Steiningen was thrown down and killed by treading on his long beard on the staircase leading to the council-chamber of Brunn. The long beard of John Mayo, a painter in Germany, is matter of history; he used to untie it in the presence of Charles V., who laughed heartily on seeing it blown about in the faces of the courtiers. Busbequius saw at Constantinople a janissary with such a quantity of hair on his head that a musket-ball would not penetrate it: we suspect there was some legerdemain in this case, and that the celebrated wizard was anticipated in his gun trick by some two hundred years or more. Some commentators have endeavoured to determine the weight of Absalom's long and beautiful hair, but they differ widely in their computation; we are told that when its inconvenient length compelled him at times to cut it off it was found to weigh 200 shekels, which Geddes estimates at 112 ounces, and Clarke at 7-1/2 ounces—a conclusion in which nothing is concluded. Seven to eight ounces is held to be about the average weight of a lady's tresses. With those who shave the beard its growth is said to be at the rate of six and a half inches per annum, so that in forty years a man must have cut off rather more than twenty feet of beard.

In the natural course, when the hair has attained a certain growth, it is thrown off, and its place supplied by a new growth formed from the pulp within the hair follicle. This process is continually going on, and is analogous to the shedding of the coat in quadrupeds, or the moulting of birds at certain seasons. The German physiologists, whose arduous and persevering labours in scientific research have never been excelled, have investigated with rare industry the minutest details respecting the growth of the hair; and one of them has accomplished the task of counting the number of hairs in heads of four different colours. In a blond one he found 140,000 hairs; in a brown, 109,440; in a black, 102,962; and in a red one, 88,740. Erasmus Wilson states that the superficial surface of the scalp may be taken at 120 inches, he averages the number of hairs per inch at 1000, which gives 120,000 for the entire head. It will be seen from the greater fineness of the blond hairs that the number is greater than those of red or black hair, and that red is the coarsest. The silken fineness of some shades of light hair is very remarkable, even the poets are evidently put to their wits end adequately to express its extreme fineness and beauty,—it is likened to the golden beams of day—and who has not seen the light playing upon it, and streaming rays and sparkles of lustrous beauty given out, as it were, from a diffused wave of sunshine—

"And on her hair a glory, like a saint."

It is not clearly shown to what we must attribute the disposition to curl, which some hair naturally possesses. Some have thought that it was owing in a great measure to the presence of a considerable amount of oily matter in the shaft of the hair, which hinders the animal matter from attracting moisture which would have a tendency, it is said, to straighten the hair. But the more probable and more general opinion is that it mainly arises from the flatness of the hair. Now this flattening is sometimes very considerable, and the diameter of the hair two-thirds broader in one direction than in the other. The hair of the beard and whiskers exhibits the peculiarity most distinctly. In proportion to its size, the strength of a hair is very remarkable; one from a boy supported a weight of 7,812 grains; another from a man, 14,285 grains. The elasticity of the hair is very apparent, a hair 10 inches long has been stretched to 13 inches; and a hair stretched one-fifth of its entire length returns, with but trifling excess, to its first dimensions.

The chemical analysis of human hair, as given by Liebig, shows that its constituents are carbon, hydrogen, nitrogen, oxygen, and sulphur. Fair hair contains most sulphur and oxygen, and the least carbon and hydrogen; black hair the most carbon and hydrogen, and the least sulphur and oxygen. The hair of the beard contains more carbon and less sulphur than the hair of the head. The presence of sulphur occasions the peculiar odour of burnt hair, but we question the fact, as stated by some authors, that red hair is perceptibly redolent of brimstone. By experiments, Vauquelin obtained from black hair a whitish and a greyish oil; the whitish oil was also present in red hair, but the place of the greyish green oil was supplied by an oil; the colour of blood. Hair is one of the most indestructible of animal substances, even less perishable than the bones; this arises from the small quantity of water it contains, its chief bulk being made up of various salts of lime, iron, and manganese. In mummies more than two thousand years old the hair has been found unaltered, as may be seen in our own and other public museums. In the Abbey Church of Romsey, the hair of a female apparently of the time of the Normans was found perfectly entire on opening a coffin in 1839. It is in plaits 18-inches long, and preserved in a glass case, lying upon the same block of oak which has been its pillow for centuries. And somewhat recently, when the tombs of Gustavus Vasa and his Queen Gunilla, in the Cathedral at Upsal, were explored to gratify the longings of some worthy antiquaries; the hair of the Queen, which according to the popular annals was of extraordinary beauty, still remained—when ought else of earthly beauty had perished in the grave.

Hair is a non-conductor of electricity, and every one is familiar with the experiment illustrating electrical repulsion, which causes

> "The knotted and combined locks to part,
>
> And each particular hair to stand on end
>
> Like quills upon the fretful porcupine."

Some persons possess the power of giving considerable motion to the scalp, and in moments of excitement do so involuntarily with some curious results—as was witnessed by Haydon at one of the readings given by Mrs. Siddons. The artist sat behind an old gentleman with his hair tied in a queue, which suddenly rose like a knocker, and continued the most lively movements during an interval of intense and breathless attention on the part of the audience. A good ghost-story will sometimes electrify a youngster, and convert the curled darling into a regular Brutus. In the "May of life," e'er he had "supped full with horrors," Macbeth himself had felt such innocent fears:

> "The time has been, my senses would have cool'd
>
> To hear a night-shriek; and my fell of hair
>
> Would at a dismal treatise rouse, and stir
>
> As life were in't."

But does the hair grow after death? Most persons who have not reflected a little on the question, answer readily in the affirmative. The contraction of the cuticle after death, which causes an apparent lengthening of the beard, has by many been mistaken for a new growth of hair. But there are strange instances on record, where, on entering the charnel house, a coffin has been found to be completely covered with an extraordinary growth of hair-like filaments issuing from chinks in the wood or metal, and trailing in every direction to a distance of some feet. Such a phenomenon is truly wonderful, account for it what way you will. The common solution of the difficulty supposes the hair to have grown to this enormous length, and to have been nourished in some way by organic elements resulting from decomposition. We need not stop to refute this. The opinion which inclines to its being of vegetable growth is likely enough to find favour with those who have seen the remarkable and beautiful parasites which clothe with their fantastic draperies the recesses of mines and caverns. But this we will leave to learned professors to settle among themselves.

The colouring principle in the hair and skin is held to be of a like nature. Light hair usually accompanies a fair complexion, and black hair a dark one; and every gradation from fair to dark is generally marked by a corresponding alteration in the tint of the hair. The colour of the skin and hair being one of the physical characters which serve to distinguish the several races of mankind, we may divide them into two great groups: the fair-haired and the dark-haired races. The dark-haired race occupies by far the greater portion of the globe; the light-haired race being restricted comparatively to a few settlements, chiefly in Europe, and more especially its northern region. These fair-haired races of the North, in their bold descents upon the British coasts and subsequent immigrations, drove the dark-haired Celts and Cymri from the plains back upon their mountain strongholds, and completely dispossessed the indigenous tribes of their territory. From the intermixture of race we derive that obvious variety in the different shades of hair which characterizes the mixed population of this country—a diversity which contributes not a little to the remarkable beauty of the women of Great Britain—while the intermixture of race has doubtless stamped that daring and energy upon the people which have made these isles the Palladium of Liberty and the envy of the world. We notice some marked peculiarities among certain tribes in respect to the colour and character of the hair. The Mongols and Northern Asiatics, for instance, are scantily furnished with hair and beard; the Kurilians, on the contrary, are said to be the most hairy race of people in the world. Their beards hang upon their breasts, and arms, neck and back are covered with hair. Some of the Esquimaux have so much beard upon the face that it is difficult to make out their features. The Incas of South America, with long thick hair, very soft and straight, have only a few scanty hairs for a beard. The North American Indians have straight lank hair. The

African Negroes, woolly hair, which, it is needless to say, is very different from wool, being merely hair in a peculiar state of crispness. The colouring matter in the hair of the Negro is in much greater quantity than in the European. Sometimes this woolly hair is met with of great length; a tribe of Negroes on the Gold Coast have woolly hair fully half a yard long, which is usually black, but red hair is not uncommon. The Papuas of New Guinea have long black frizzled hair growing in tufts in the most strange but admired disorder, which makes their heads appear of enormous size. The Cafusos in the Brazils, known to have sprung from the native Americans and the Negroes from Africa, have their hair excessively long, half woolly and curly at the ends, rising eighteen inches or more perpendicularly from the scalp, forming a very ugly and ridiculous kind of wig: the wearers are obliged to stoop as they go in and out of their huts, and the mass of hair is so entangled that it is impossible to comb it. The Chinese have very little beard, although extremely anxious to make the most of it. Some tribes are at great pains to eradicate the beard, and a tribe of Indians on the Coppermine River not only pluck out the beard, but pull out the hairs from the head, thus realizing the condition of the Myconians, who, says Pliny, have naturally no hair at all. Generally speaking, the coloured races are most wanting in beard, and the white races most liberally furnished therewith. In the Albino, the hair is of the palest flaxen or a dull whitish hue, and the colouring matter altogether wanting; the skin partakes of the same deadly paleness, and the pupils of the eyes are of a pink colour. Albinoes cannot endure a strong light; when exposed to the light, the eyelids are half closed and continually blinking. In disposition, the Albinoes are gentle and not deficient in intellect. This peculiar variety was first noticed among the blacks, and obtained the name of *white negroes*. But Albinoes, it is known, are not confined to any particular race or country. In some Africans, patches of white hair are seen covering portions of the head, and in those parts the skin is invariably white.

That the colour of the hair in certain races has undergone a considerable change in the course of time is apparent from what is known to have taken place in Britain. The ancient Germans were universally characterized by red hair and blue eyes, and what is termed a strongly marked zanthous constitution; but, Niebuhr says, the Germans are now far from being a light-haired race; and Chevalier Bunsen remarks that he has often looked in vain for the golden or auburn locks and light cærulean eyes of the old Germans among their descendants, but in Scandinavia he found the colour of the hair and eyes precisely those described by Tacitus. From this it is inferred that the altered conditions of life, brought about by civilization, have produced a change in the physical character of the people. Such change, however, is confined within very narrow limits; in the hair it is but a mere shade of colour or variation in its crispness. Under the microscope, the definite form of the human hair is most exact and uniform; so much so, that Mr. Queckett was enabled by this test to confirm the conjectures of the Archæological Society, in a very scientific manner, respecting some portions of skin taken from church doors in Essex, and from Worcester Cathedral. Tradition said, pirates and persons guilty of sacrilege in old time were flayed, and their skins nailed to the church door. Mr. Queckett was to determine if the relics confided to his charge, and which looked exactly like scraps of old parchment, were really portions of the human body. A few hairs were discovered adhering to the skin and this decided the point—it was unmistakeably human hair and human skin—and the Archæologists were made happy by the discovery. Would that we could send the smallest fragment of one of those skins with but a solitary hair upon it—which Hanno hung up in the Temple of Juno— to Mr. Q., with the publishers' compliments, that he might ascertain the true character of the hairy people the old Carthaginian fell in with on his route.

The colour of the hair is also an indication of temperament: black hair is usually accompanied by a bilious temperament; fair and auburn, with the sanguine and sanguine-nervous; and very light hair, with a temperament mild and lymphatic.

Will any one undertake to say what was the precise colour of the golden hair so vaunted of by the great poets of antiquity? One of our living poets, the author of "The Bride of Rimini," has brought the light of genius and his fine taste and scholarship to the task, and the matter is yet doubtful. Some have not hesitated to decide that it was red, fiery red, and nothing short of red; and sneered at the ancients for affecting to be connoisseurs in these things. Some have contended that it was auburn, which is a glorious colour, and seems naturally associated with smiles and the rich imagery of poets. In the well-known ode of Anacreon, where he speaks of the beauty of his mistress as a fit subject for the painter's art, it is difficult to say what colour we must choose. Some prefer to think dark jetty locks were intended, such, possibly, as Byron has given to one of his beauties:

> "The glossy darkness of that clustering hair,
>
> Which shades, yet shows a forehead more than fair."

Ben Jonson—no mean authority—blends with the jetty locks threads of fine gold:

> "Gold upon a ground of black."

If a mere stripling might handle the bow of Ulysses, we would venture to select the colour which Tennyson has bestowed upon a pretty little portrait:

"Her eyes a bashful azure, and her hair

In gloss and hue the chesnut, when the shell

Divides threefold to show the fruit within."

But why be beholden to poets, who, after all, are but the interpreters of nature? Does not Scotland to this day own many a fair complexion, and tresses which Venice cannot match for sunny splendour; and are not the dark, flowing locks of the Lancashire witches working as secret charms as ever enthralled the courteous knights of old? It is certain that, in regard to the hair, the ancients had no monopoly of beauty.

Concerning grey hair, we may remark that the term is a misnomer applied to single hairs; for the greyness merely arises from the commingling of white and dark hairs. When the secretion of the colouring matter in the pulp ceases, all succeeding growth from the bulb is colourless. Every one feels some little anxiety about grey hairs. To the moralist they are Death's blossoms—the solemn warning to adjust the mantle e'er we fall. With some, grey hairs will even intrude upon the pleasures of youth; with others, they are but as the ripening of the corn—when wisdom gathers her full harvest against the time of declining strength; again, in others, they wait upon old age, like a wreath of snow on the brow of winter; and some enjoy life to its fullest span, and there is no sign of "the sere and yellow leaf:" so various are the conditions of life which produce the change of constitution which accompanies grey hairs. It is amusing to notice the special theory which each one contrives to account for the presence of these tell-tales. "Ah!" said Louis XII., as he looked in the mirror, somewhat astonished at the number of grey hairs, "these are owing to the long speeches I have listened to, those especially of M. le——, have ruined my hair." It was mere folly for the Teian bard to tell the girls how prettily the white hairs of age contrast with the rich tresses of youth, like roses and lilies in a chaplet, or milk upon roses; for at his time of life, the old Sybarite ought to have known better. We remember to have felt deeply for the unfortunate bridegroom, when we first read the tragical story, in the Encyclopædia Metropolitana, of the gentleman, "who, at his marriage, when about forty years old, had a dark head of hair; but, on his return from his wedding trip, had become so completely snow white, even to his eyebrows, that his friends almost doubted his identity." Even the curled Anthony must needs make excuses to the fair Egyptian for his grey hairs:

"What, girl? though grey

Do something mingle with our younger brown;

Yet ha' we a brain that nourishes our nerves,

And can get goal for goal of youth."

How sudden grief and consuming care will blanch the hair is known to all. Memory recalls the lone prisoner in the castle of Chillon, and the lofty queen who passed from a throne to a prison and the scaffold, to teach heroes how to face death. And by these truthful signs, these silver hairs, may oftentimes be traced the story of a broken heart—of hope too long deferred—of fallen ambition—of blighted affection, or of man's ingratitude. What more sacred than these secret sorrows; who would seek to pry into them with idle questionings? The leaf is withered, for the worm is at the heart of the tree:

> "This white top writeth mine oldé years;
>
> Mine heart is also mouldered as mine hairs."

But hope and sunshine gather about the grey hairs ripe for immortality:

> "Thy silver locks, once auburn bright,
>
> Are still more lovely in my sight
>
> Than golden beams of orient light,
>
> > My Mary."

We have hitherto regarded the hair as a thing of beauty and the crowning ornament of man's structure. We have now to consider the diseases to which it is subject; and first we will speak of Baldness. Where partial baldness arises from debility of the system, the growth of hair usually follows on restoration to health, and accidental baldness may generally be removed by the ordinary applications. But the baldness of a more permanent character, which results from the obliteration of the hair-follicles, seldom admits of a perfect remedy. In such cases the skin is smooth and glossy, as is duly noted by Chaucer, in his portrait of the monk:

> "His head was bald, and shone as any glass."

This is the alopecia of pathologists, so called because it was said foxes were especially subject to baldness; or, as some think to express, by way of irony, that cunning and duplicity may be looked for in bald men. The ridicule and contempt which the ancients heaped upon these unfortunate individuals is very obvious. Among the Hebrews the term bald-pate was an insult and a reproach. The origin of this appears to have been that baldness was held to be the sign of a corrupt youth and a dissolute life. And when physiologists are asked to certify to the falsehood of such calumnies, they answer in riddles like the Sphinx.

"Turpe pecus mutilum, turpis sine gramine campus

Et sine fronde frutex, et sine crine caput."

The ancients were so proud of their curls and flowing locks, the physical beauty of manhood, and the charms of their female deities, earthly and celestial, that, for the sake of antithesis it may be, they hurled their sarcasms and their sneers with a savage vengeance or ignoble pity upon their bald-pated victims in a style which modern politeness declines to imitate. It is surprising that Cæsar should have shown such sensitiveness about his baldness as to have sought permission of the Senate to wear his laurel crown at pleasure. The privilege was granted, and the laurels shaded the bald pate. Fortunately women are so very rarely bald that we may consider them exempt from this infliction. Apuleius, in his Melesiacs, says, that Venus herself, if she were bald, though surrounded by the Graces and the Loves, could not be pleasing even to her husband, Vulcan. Herodotus remarked that few Egyptians were bald; and eunuchs, who have much subcutaneous fat about the scalp, are free from baldness. It may be some consolation to bachelors to know, that according to Pliny man in a state of single blessedness is never bald. Caligula and Nero are numbered among the bald, and kings have been honored with the title. Baldness has even found panegyrists. Synesius, bishop of Syrene, in the fifteenth century, wrote in praise of it; and Hucbald, a Benedictine monk, made it the subject of a curious poem, which he very appropriately dedicated to Charles the Bald. But these perverse eulogists were ecclesiastics who reckoned the beauty of the hair and its enticements part of the vanities of this wicked world it would be well to get rid of. Happily the hair escaped their treacherous shears. It is possible, however, to have too much of a good thing; and the excessive growth of hair where least wanted is numbered among the ills which flesh is heir to. No one in these days would think the King of Persia's porter, seen by Tavernier, deserved a double pension because he could tie his moustaches behind his neck; for something very like this may be seen any afternoon in Hyde Park; there is a fashion in such things, and Nature is by no means niggardly in her gifts to man. But what is meant by an extraneous growth of hair is very different from this, and by no means ornamental. We allude to cases where the whole body has been covered by a growth of long hair. Some miserable Fakirs, in India, have been seen clothed with hair several inches long. About 1650, a hairy child was shown as a sight, and the strange phenomenon is thus accounted for in an old play:

"'Tis thought the hairy child that's shewn about,

Came by the mother's thinking on the picture

Of St. John Baptist in his camel's coat."

But the most frightful instances are those of bearded women. "I like not when a 'oman has a great peard," says Sir Hugh; and the old naturalists are at some pains to assure us that woman is not barbigerous, for which a very sufficient reason has been given:

"Nature, regardful of the babbling race,

Planted no beard upon a woman's face;

Not MAPPIN'S razors, though the very best,

Could shave a chin which never is at rest."

One of the best known examples of this repulsive class, (Trifaldi, the afflicted Duenna not excepted), is that of Barbara Urselin, born at Augsburg, and shown in Ratcliffe Highway, in 1668; her portrait may be seen in Granger's Biography, and Evelyn takes note of her in his Journal. Her face and hands were all over hairy, the hair on her forehead and eyebrows combed upwards, she had a long spreading beard, the hair of which hung loose and flowing like the hair of the head. A fellow of the name of Van Beck married the frightful creature to carry about as a show. Charles XII. had in his army a female grenadier, who had both the beard and the courage of a man. She was taken prisoner at the battle of Pultowa, and carried to St. Petersburg, where she was presented to the Czar; her beard measured a yard and a half. In 1852, a young woman, a native of Switzerland, with beard and whiskers four inches long, could find no clergyman to marry her to the object of her affections, until provided with a certificate from Charing Cross Hospital. Many other authentic cases are on record, but the subject is not inviting.

In rare instances, the colour of the hair undergoes a strange metamorphosis from red to black, or it may be from brown to blue or green, and sometimes it has been seen spotted like the leopard's skin. Instances are known in which it became so sensitive that the slightest touch caused exquisite pain. Sometimes the hair splits at the point, and becomes forked. There is also, the very rare disease—plica Polonica—originating, no doubt, in filth and neglect, in which the hair becomes inextricably tangled and matted together by a glutinous fluid from the roots, and the hairs when cut are said to bleed. In the Museum of the College of Surgeons, the hair of a cat may be seen exhibiting all the peculiarities of this singular disease. The elf-locks of the old chieftains which Scott describes:—

"His plaited hair in elf locks spread

Around his bare and matted head—"

and the locks which Queen Mab and the Fairies are accused of weaving "in foul sluttish hairs," are no doubt symptoms of the same diseased and monstrous plaiting.

That the hair is any standard of physical strength is one of those popular notions which rest on no sufficient data. Samson's strength was the direct gift of God—

"God when he gave me strength, to show withal

How slight the gift was, hung it in my hair."

Nisus' life was held by the singular tenure of one golden or purple hair, which grew on the top of his head; this was plucked by the hand of his unnatural daughter and his life fell a sacrifice to her craft: so runs the tale. We cannot say if hearts are still held in fief by the gift of a lock of hair, or if lovers in this stern iron-age recognize the old traditions in their love affairs; but broad lands were conveyed in other days by as slight a bond. The Earl of Warren, in the reign of Henry III., confirmed to the church of S. Pancras, at Lewes, certain land, rent, and tithe, of which he gave seisin *per Capillos capitis sui et fratis sui Radulfi*; and the hair of the parties was cut off by the Bishop of Winchester before the high altar.

The hair, from its imperishable nature, constitutes a material link between the living and the dead; it survives in form and beauty as when it graced the brows of the living; unchanged in death, it shares in the lasting homage which we gladly pay to the memory of the brave and the good. Who can regard with indifference the sacred relics preserved at Penshurst—the locks of hair of Sir Philip and Algernon Sidney? Leigh Hunt has other like-treasured memorials, of which an account has been given to the public by an American author. The locks are those of Milton, Keats, Shelley, Charles Lamb, Dr. Johnson, Swift; and the poet may well feel proud to own them.

From what has been said respecting the growth of the hair, it will be perceived that there are some special points to be attended to, if we would keep it in perfect order. As the hair rises from the bulb above the cuticle, it carries with it a thin pellicle, which adheres for a time to the shaft, and afterwards falls off in minute scales, and forms a kind of scurf in the hair. Now, this is simply a natural process, and not to be mistaken for a diseased state of the skin; the scales of detached film merely require to be removed with the brush and comb. Very different, however, are the scales on the skin of the head, which, at times, form a loose dandriff, filling the hair with a most unsightly scurf. This is a serious evil, and requires patient and careful treatment to get rid of thoroughly; and nothing can be less likely to effect a remedy than the use of very hard brushes, which, by irritating the scalp, tend to aggravate the symptoms. Anything which unnaturally irritates the skin of the head will originate dandriff; when the functions of the excretory pores and sebaceous glands are interrupted, the skin becomes dry, and the cuticle may be said partially to perish; the dead particles are then thrown off by cuticular exfoliation. Above all, extreme cleanliness, constant and habitual attention to the purity of the skin, are the best curatives, and the only safeguard against the occurence of this very simple, but troublesome and obstinate disease of the cuticle. The most disagreeable circumstance to be noted in this complaint is, that those who should enjoy perfect immunity from the annoyance,—those

"Who have but fed on the roses, and lain in the lilies of life"—

by the use of stimulant pomatums, improper hair-brushes, and badly made combs, but chiefly the use of abominable nostrums—not unfrequently entail upon themselves the very evils which are commonly produced by the opposite means, neglect and inattention to the state of the hair. The hair requires but a moderate supply of pommade; but this, to be of any real benefit, must be compounded *secundem artem*, and adapted to the purpose. Oils and pomatums which merely collect dust are not to be tolerated, and are frequently had recourse to merely to disguise the neglect which suffers the hair to become rough from being in ill-condition. Whenever proper attention is given to the hair, the most satisfactory results are usually obtained; and without bestowing such an amount of care, it is impossible to realize the beautiful softness and lustre which any lady's tresses may be made to assume. It cost the poet little to bring together

"Love-darting eyes, and tresses like the morn;"

but we promise none but very ordinary tresses to such as will not, both night and morn, with brush and comb, and suitable preparation, detach every particle of dust from the hair. And to those who can appreciate the beautiful, and would gratify a more refined feeling than mere personal vanity, the disposition of the hair affords an admirable opportunity of setting off, by the graces of art, "the beauty of a woman's face"—

"Angels are painted fair, to look like you."

All the canons of criticism are summed up in the perfections of female beauty. What greater ornament to perfect beauty that luxuriant hair? We will conclude our advice to the fair with some old verses of Richard Lovelace, which express, with the freedom of a poet, a truth that might take the form of an aphorism, that the beauty of the hair consists in its flowing outline, its flexibility, and varying tints—the effect of light reflected from its glossy surface:

> "Amarantha, sweet and fair,
>
> Oh, braid no more that shining hair!
>
> Let it fly, as unconfin'd
>
> As its calm ravisher, the wind;
>
> Who hath left his darling, th' east,
>
> To wanton o'er that spicy nest.
>
> Every tress must be confest,
>
> But neatly tangled, at the best;
>
> Like a clue of golden thread
>
> Most excellently ravelled.
>
> Do not, then, wind up the light
>
> In ribands, and o'ercloud in night,
>
> Like the sun's in early ray;
>
> But shake your head, and scatter day!"

THE END.

Milton Keynes UK
Ingram Content Group UK Ltd.
UKHW040311181024
449757UK00005B/495